LEARNING KOREAN
WITH A SMILE

VOCABULARY

EASY VOCABULARY MEMORIZATION

이 도서의 국립중앙도서관 출판시도서목록(CIP)은 서지정보유통지원시스템 홈페이지(http://seoji.nl.go.kr)와 국가자료공동목록시스템(http://www.nl.go.kr/kolisnet)에서 이용하실수 있습니다. (CIP제어번호 : CIP2016010278)

LEARNING KOREAN WITH A SMILE

WITH A SMILE

VOCABULARY

EASY VOCABULARY MEMORIZATION

ADRIAN PERRIG

MIYOUNG JUNG

YEON YIM

HEEJO LEE

Für Stefan Perrig - Adrian Perrig

스테판 페릭 형을 위해 – 아드리안 페릭

For Bong Seob Shin - Miyoung Jung

사랑하는 엄마께 – 정미영

For Chang Joon Yim - Yeon Yim

아버지께 – 임정연

To my parents in a peach orchard - Heejo Lee

엄마, 아빠 사랑해요 – 이희조

We are looking forward to hearing comments and suggestions on how to further improve this book series. With your encouragement and support, we anticipate to publish a complete set of Korean study books, to enable you to study the language with a smile!

For comments & suggestions
Email us at : info@smile-korean.com
Visit us at : www.smile-korean.com

CONTENTS

INTRODUCTION

Are you having trouble learning Korean vocabulary? You are seeing the same word again and again but you cannot remember it?

This book is to learn Korean vocabulary with the goal to learn as many useful Korean words in as short time and as enjoyable manner as possible. By building up a solid base vocabulary, one can rapidly progress to master the language.

This book is recommended to be used in conjunction with a standard course in Korean that teaches grammar and conversation. The novelty of this book is to use a combination of advanced memorization techniques to make it as easy as possible to memorize and retain Korean vocabulary. In fact, this book is the 2nd book in the 4-book series "Learning Korean with a Smile": reading & writing, vocabulary, grammar, conversation. The grammar and conversation books are forthcoming.

We assume that the reader is already familiar with reading and pronouncing Hangeul. If not, we recommend reading our book "Learning Korean with a Smile: Reading & Writing". For words with difficult pronunciations, we will use markers to refer to the pronunciation rule in our reading & writing book. For example: sliding door 미닫이 is pronounced as 미다지, following Pronunciation Rule 1.2 from our previous book, so we will write 미닫이[mi-da-ji][PR1.2].

The reason why we developed this book with a number of advanced memorization techniques is because one of the authors tried to learn Korean with conventional techniques and encountered significant difficulties.

Korean turns out to be a very difficult language

for non-native Korean speakers, requiring special study aids to make it possible to learn it without an abundance of frustration and tears. The core difficulties for the vocabulary stem from the fact that Korean is very different from Western languages. It is often very hard to form associations between Korean and English words. One could say the same of other Asian languages. A particular challenge also shared by Japanese and Vietnamese, is that Korean uses words derived from Chinese characters (called Sino-Korean) and from original Korean (called pure Korean) for the same concept, which have their respective specific uses. This can be overwhelming for the Korean learner, but fortunately, we have identified patterns and have disentangled the concepts to present notions in a simple manner to avoid tears and retain a smile for the learner.

We follow a multi-faceted learning approach

in this book.

First, we provide a historical background of the Korean language to describe the origin of Korean words — with many influences from China, Japan, and India over the past 2000 years, and many recent influences from other Western languages, especially English.

Second, we group words that share a similar context to provide an easy manner to study. To simplify the study, we find that redundancy through repetition is desirable: tomato appears both in the section on loan words and in the section on vegetables.

Third, we present loan words from other languages, which are especially simple for learners proficient in a Western language. Examples words are "elevator" 엘레베이터 and "computer" 컴퓨터.

Fourth, we find that association-based learning is particularly powerful to master Korean. In our own experience, learning Korean vocabulary is a long and arduous process. Association-based learning is a formidable vehicle for memory retention — speeding up learning similar to speeding up transportation by using a bicycle or car as compared to walking. By providing intuitive associations for numerous words, we hope that you will share our excitement and rapid progress this technique provides. Below, we will further elaborate on association-based learning.

Fifth, and finally, we present Sino-Korean and pure Korean based prefixes and suffixes. As numerous Sino-Korean words are composed by Sino-Korean prefixes and suffixes, the knowledge of these word stems greatly simplifies learning by enabling the formation of associations between the meaning of the word and the meaning of the word stems. As we find the retention of Sino-Korean words particularly challenging, the knowledge of the word stems has been particularly helpful.

책
[chaeg]

서
[seo]

For example, '책[chaeg]' is a pure Korean word and '서[seo]' is a Sino-Korean affix both meaning 'book.' While '책[chaeg]' is used independently as a casual word, '서[seo]' is used when making more complex words related to books such as 독서[dog-seo] "reading" or 도서관[do-seo-gwan] "library."

We have decided to omit extensive lists of hundreds of verbs and adjectives (along with their conjugation), as they will be more naturally introduced in the forthcoming grammar and conversation books. Similarly, words for different politeness levels will be taught in the grammar and conversation books as well.

Unfortunately, most Korean words make no inherent sense, as there is absolutely no similarity to the corresponding English word. Studying can thus be frustrating: the first few words are easy, but once you try to memorize several dozens of words they all start to mingle up in one's mind forming a magnificent mess.

Association-based learning techniques for easier memorization, along with a staged repetition system have proven to dramatically improve language learning. These techniques are to learning Korean words like martial arts to fighting: with some simple technique one is much more effective! We will now introduce these techniques in more detail.

꽃
[ggot]

goat

To remember 꽃 "flower", imagine a goat eating a flower!

ASSOCIATION-BASED LEARNING

Consider this simple observation: if something makes intuitive sense, it is much easier to remember than some random information. For example, if the PIN code of your bank card is the same as the birthday of your spouse, then all you need to do is to associate the bank card with your spouse and you will have an easy time to remember the code. This exemplifies the power of association.

Brain researchers have found that the human brain has the ability to memorize an almost unlimited number of associations. We can use this fact and form associations between a similar-sounding word we know and the corresponding Korean word we want to learn. This is best described with an example. The Korean word for 1000 is '천 [cheon],' and we can remember the sentence "the city has

1000 people named JOHN". So you form an association of the number 1000 with "the city of 1000 Johns". Similarly, the Korean word for 10000 is '만 [man],' which you can associate with "this MAN has 10000 friends on Facebook". The Korean word for 100 million is '억 [eog],' which you can associate with "I have 100 million OAK trees". Easy, isn't it?

Association techniques are more memorable if you come up with a vivid picture in your mind. It is suggested that you invent some funny or even crazy pictures, which seem to form a stronger association. The more vivid, colorful, and innovative the better. So it may take about 15 seconds to come up with a vivid picture and imagine it, but this is much faster and more pleasant than repeating a word 20 to 30 times and then still forgetting it. Unless you're a language genius, you may recall instances where you have seen a word over 20 times and your brain simply refused to memorize it. After forming an association, you will be likely to immediately remember it! Thanks to associations, you will be able to learn Korean with a smile. ☺

Good associations can be hard to come up with. You will get better at it over time. In this book, we will give you many associations for difficult-to-remember words, all you need to do is to come up with a colorful picture in your mind to memorize it.

PURE KOREAN vs SINO-KOREAN

For many words, Korean has a word with a Korean root and another word with a Chinese root, they are called "pure Korean" and "Sino-Korean" words, respectively. It can be a bit confusing, as they mean the same but only one is correct to be used in a given context. A good example is the pure Korean and Sino-Korean numbers. Yes, indeed, there is a pure Korean and a corresponding Sino-Korean word for 1, 2, 3, etc.

To aid memorization, we propose a triple-association for each word, where we associate a little girl for pure Korean and a Panda bear for Sino-Korean words. For the case of numbers, we use the number-rhyme system to associate an object with each number, for example, "hen" is associated with "ten". So then we form an association of the Panda bear, a hen, and a ship by imagining the Panda bear with hens on a SHIP, and then you can easily remember the Sino-Korean word for 10 which is 십 [ship]. When you form the association of the little girl and the hens you imagine the little girl stating "I love YOU ALL" and you can remember the pure Korean word for 10 which is 열 [yeol]. It may sound a bit complicated at first, but for most learners, this is going to save a lot of grief and tears.

This all sounds too good to be true, right? There must be some hook... Well actually, in this case it is as good as it sounds. Of course, you can forget associations and you may thus need to repeat them. But we hope to dispel other concerns.

One concern is: Is this going to mess up my brain? Will I forever have an association between the number 1000 and a city of 1000

Johns? Is this somehow going to harm my thought process? Fortunately, the association is like a training wheel on a bicycle. When you first start bicycling as a child, the training wheels prevent numerous bruises and ensure that you can start bicycling with a smile. Later, you do not use the training wheels any more and surely you do not miss them at all. Similar with associations, when you need to recall a word, the association can help you. But as soon as you internalize the word, it will come to you naturally and you will not need the association any more. Because you don't use the association any more, you will naturally forget it. It's as simple as that.

What if I want to learn another language, will the associations interfere? Yes, they may actually interfere, so we don't recommend to simultaneously learn several languages with associations.

Do I need to form an association with every word I ever want to learn? For many words, they may stick in your mind without associations. If you're a language genius, you can simply pile up the words in your brain for easy retrieval. But for us mortals, many words are difficult and need an association to memorize. Hopefully, after some time, the word will become natural and the association is not needed any more.

Is this going to be too slow and impractical to speak? Indeed, it can be a bit slow to retrieve a word with an association. However, recall the training wheel analogy, the more you practice the word, the quicker it will become memorized and the sooner you can toss the training wheels.

STAGED REPETITION SYSTEMS

How to study? Should we study in the morning or in the evening? Should we study in a quiet place, when you're waiting in a line, or when you're on the move in a bus? How often should you repeat the words you have mastered: after one, two, or even 7 days?

These are all important questions, but they don't have a simple answer because each person has a different learning style. Some can learn only in quiet places, while others require noise around them to concentrate, so you need to find out what works best for you. However, for everyone a staged repetition system is crucial for long-term retention.

In fact, when we first learn a word, it is only retained in short-term memory. To copy the word to intermediate-term memory, we need to repeat the word after 1-3 days. Similarly, to copy the word from intermediate-term memory to long-term memory, we need to repeat it again after 1-2 weeks. Once the word is in long-term memory, we only need to refresh it every couple of months for it to stay there.

Although each person is different, for most people daily practice is important, even if it's just for a few minutes.

So how can we implement a staged repetition system? The simplest approach is to use flash cards. You look at the first card and it may say "every day" on it — you try to remember the corresponding Korean word which is "매일[mae-il]". If you remember "매일" well, you can simply put the card all the way to the back of the stack. But if you have trouble remembering the word, you can place the card closer to the front of the stack so that you'll see it again within a few minutes. Automagically, you rehearse the words you know less well more often. In this method, the flash card stack automatically implements a staged repetition system. We very much encourage you to use such flash cards for words you have trouble with, it can work wonders!

You can also write your association on the flash card, in order to remember challenging associations.

We also recommend flashcard applications for mobile devices such as Android or iPhone smart phones. One application we have made good experiences with is called Anki, it's free on Android, and allows downloading free Korean flash cards.

SYMBOLS USED IN THIS BOOK

Below is a list of icons each representing the grammatical category of a word. They will be placed on the left side of word tables in Chapters 2 - 12.

N = nouns

Aj = adjectives

V = verbs

Av = adverbs

Nu = numerals

Pr = prepositions

C = conjunctions

In = interjections

Af = affixes

On the right side of the word table, you will see some pronunciations with special 'Pronunciation Rule' marks in superscript letters such as: [pronunciation]$^{PR\ Number}$. You can find the correct pronunciation tips by following the rule numbers in 'Chapter 5' in our 'Learning Korean with a Smile: Reading & Writing' book.

Together with English and Korean words, the word table looks like this:

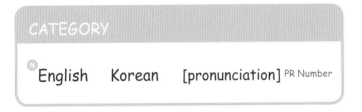

CATEGORY		
English	Korean	[pronunciation] $^{PR\ Number}$

And now... let's get started!

Starting with a brief history of
Korean philosophies and
religions,
we can understand
how Korean vocabulary was
formed
over the past 4000 years.

HISTORY OF KOREAN
VOCABULARY

(1) OVERVIEW

Korean is the official language of South Korea and North Korea. It is also one of the two official languages of the Yanbian Korean Autonomous Prefecture in China. Approximately 80 million people speak Korean as the 11th most frequently spoken language in the world.

More people start to learn Korean due to the increase in popularity of South Korean culture with the so-called Korean Wave or Hallyu. The Korean Wave was first driven by Korean TV dramas (K-dramas) broadcast across East and Southeast Asia since the early 2000s. The Korean Wave evolved into a global phenomenon due to the proliferation of Korean pop (K-pop) music videos on YouTube.

Psy's music video for "Gangnam Style"

became the first to reach more than a billion YouTube views. Multi-billion views of Korean pop songs including Psy's on Youtube made K-pop a separate music genre. Our book can help you learn Korean with a smile and enjoy K-pop and Korean culture with more intimate understanding.

From a linguistic perspective, most linguists classify Korean as part of the Altaic[1] language family which includes Turkic, Mongolic, Tungusic, and Japonic. Other linguists suggest Korean to be a language isolate, since no genealogical relationship with other languages is demonstrated clearly. A speaker of the Altaic language may find it easier to learn Korean as these languages may share some vocabulary and grammar. Nevertheless, even if you cannot speak an Altaic language you don't need to cry because modern Korean adopts a significant number of loan words, which are the words borrowed from other languages including English, French, and German. Familiar loan words widely used in Korea make learning Korean more fun!

---

1 http://en.wikipedia.org/wiki/Altaic_languages

(2) HISTORY OF
TOTEMISM & SHAMANISM

Korean history begins with the foundation of Gojoseon, meaning ancient Joseon, in 2333 B.C.E.[2] by the legendary King Dangun, the founder of the first Korean Kingdom.

Dangun's ancestry legend begins with his

---

2 B.C.E. stands for "Before the Common Era," which has the same value with B.C. that stands for "Before Christ."

grandfather Hwanin (환인; 桓因, "Lord of Heaven"). Hwanin had a son, Hwanung, who yearned to live on the earth among the valleys and the mountains. Hwanin permitted Hwanung and 3,000 followers to descend onto Baekdu Mountain, where Hwanung founded Sinsi (신시; 神市, "City of God").

A tiger and a bear prayed to Hwanung that they wanted become human. Upon hearing their prayers, Hwanung gave them 20 cloves of garlic and a bundle of mugwort, ordering them to eat only this sacred food and remain out of the sunlight for 100 days. The tiger gave up after about twenty days and left the cave. However, the bear remained and was transformed into a woman. She married Hwanung. Soon after, they got a son, Dangun (단군), who later became the king of Korea's first kingdom.[3]

---

3 http://en.wikipedia.org/wiki/Gojoseon

People say that the hidden meaning of this story is that humility and persistent effort could win over aggressiveness.

This story can be interpreted as being related to the totemic tribes of ancient Korea. Each tribe used wild animals as their symbols of spiritual messengers, and the 2 biggest & strongest tribes were the Bear-tribe and the Tiger-tribe. The Bears and Tigers used to fight each other, but at the end, all of the tribes (including the Tiger-tribe, Eagle-tribe, Deer-tribe, etc.) were unified by a gentle female leader from the Bear-tribe. She soon married a wise man and their son Dangun became famous as he founded his kingdom '고조선[Gojoseon]' in 2333 B.C.E.[4]

"Anyone shall do something good for the

---

4 http://en.wikipedia.org/wiki/Dangun

world" were his words, known to be his founding principle. It is called '홍익인간[hong-ik-in-gan]' meaning 'benefit all humankind' or 'humanitarianism.'

(3) KOREA SINCE 100 B.C.E.

Succeeding Gojoseon was the three Kingdoms period from the 1st century B.C.E. until 7th century C.E.[5] The three Kingdoms, Goguryeo, Baekje, and Silla grew to control the Korean peninsula and its northern territory Manchuria until unification by Silla in 676. In 698, Balhae was established in old territories of Goguryeo, which led to the North South States Period (698-926).

From the early 10th century, Goryeo Dynasty (918-1392) continued until the establishment of Joseon Dynasty (1392-1910). The modern name Korea was originated from the Goryeo Dynasty during which trading with nearby countries was common.

---

5 C.E. stands for "Common Era." It has the same value with A.D. which is an abbreviation for "Anno Domini" in Latin or "the year of the Lord" in English.

The first known book in the world called Jikji, a Buddhist document, was printed during the period of Goryeo, which is now preserved at the National Library of France in Paris, as the UNESCO's Memory of the World.

Jikji book

The Jikji is the oldest book printed with movable metal type in 1377, which is 78 years prior to Johannes Gutenberg's Bible. The Jikji Memory of the World Prize by UNESCO was created in 2004 to commemorate the creation of the Jikji and recognizes institutions having contributed to the preservation and accessibility of documentary heritage.

Hangeul is the official writing system of South and North Korea today, which was invented by King Sejong the Great in 1443. Before the invention of Hangeul, the adopted Chinese characters called Hanja were used for writing Korean.

Before the creation of Hanguel, the majority of people could neither read nor write: only members of the highest class were literate. Now as a concise and powerful writing system, Hangeul helps to learn and write easily and Korea has become one of the nations with the highest literacy rate in the world.

In recent history, the Korean language was influenced through political and cultural exchanges.

In 1910, the Korean Empire was annexed by Imperial Japan until the liberation in 1945. During the 36 years of the Japanese occupation of Korea, numerous Japanese words were adopted. However, most of them are not accepted as standard language today, while some of them remain as slang words.

After the liberation in 1945 from the Japanese occupation, the partition of Korea created the states of South and North Korea. The democratic South Korea, "Republic of Korea", has rapidly grown into one of the largest economies of the world.

In South Korea, the language was heavily influenced by western languages, especially by English.

On the contrary, loan words are rarely used in North Korea, but translated into pure Korean.

For example, "donut" is called 도넛[do-neot] in South Korea, 가락지빵[ka-rag-ji-bbang] in North Korea. 가락지빵 is a combined word of 가락지 (ring) and 빵(bread), which means a bread in the shape of a ring. In this way, North Korean people make a new word by combing existing words for describing distinctive features. More words are shown below.

ice cream

North → 얼음보숭이 [eo-reum-bo-sung-i]
= pile of ice

South → 아이스크림 [a-i-seu-keu-rim]

donut
- North → 가락지빵 [ka-rag-ji-bbang]
  = ring bread
- South → 도넛 [do-neot]

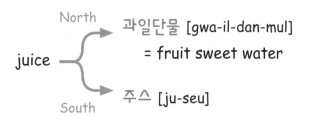

sausage
- North → 고기순대 [go-gi-sun-dae]
  = meat sausage
- South → 소시지 [so-shi-ji]

juice
- North → 과일단물 [gwa-il-dan-mul]
  = fruit sweet water
- South → 주스 [ju-seu]

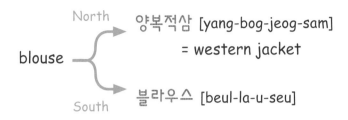

blouse
North → 양복적삼 [yang-bog-jeog-sam]
= western jacket
South → 블라우스 [beul-la-u-seu]

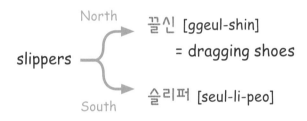

slippers
North → 끌신 [ggeul-shin]
= dragging shoes
South → 슬리퍼 [seul-li-peo]

scarf
North → 목수건 [mog-su-geon]
= neck towel
South → 스카프 [seu-ka-peu]

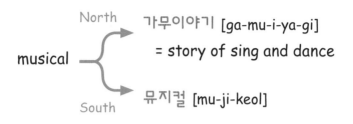

musical

North → 가무이야기 [ga-mu-i-ya-gi]
= story of sing and dance

South → 뮤지컬 [mu-ji-keol]

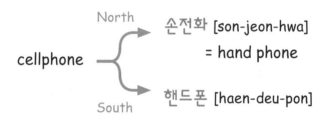

cellphone

North → 손전화 [son-jeon-hwa]
= hand phone

South → 핸드폰 [haen-deu-pon]

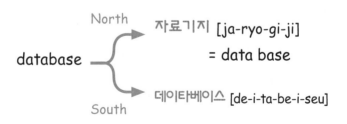

database

North → 자료기지 [ja-ryo-gi-ji]
= data base

South → 데이타베이스 [de-i-ta-be-i-seu]

South Korea imported many
new words from other languages,
especially from English.
Hence, the easiest way to learn many
Korean words is by learning how to
pronounce such loan words.
Since Hangeul cannot accurately represent
all the phonemes of Western languages, the
pronunciation is the closest equivalent to
when you try to write the word in Hangeul.
So for example, 컴퓨터 sounds like
'computer' with a Hangeul twist.

LOANWORDS

(1) LOANWORDS FROM ENGLISH

Koreans are very fashionable, and fashion continuously transforms itself. Koreans are also fashionable with their language, and English loanwords are regarded as being cool and elegant, especially when the word was recently introduced. So young Koreans often love using English loanwords, even though original Korean words are available.

This represents a nice opportunity for English speakers to kick-start their Korean vocabulary and to sound cool as an added bonus. Below, we list several categories of words.

ENGLISH LOANWORDS: FOOD

ⓝ bacon	베이컨	[be-i-keon]
ⓝ bagel	베이글	[be-i-geul]
ⓝ barbecue	바베큐	[ba-be-kyu]
ⓝ butter	버터	[beo-teo]
ⓝ cake	케익	[ke-ig]
ⓝ candy	캔디	[kaen-di]
ⓝ cereal	시리얼	[si-ri-eol]
ⓝ cheese	치즈	[chi-jeu]
ⓝ chocolate	초콜렛	[cho-kol-let]
ⓝ coffee	커피	[keo-pi]
ⓝ cookie	쿠키	[ku-ki]
ⓝ cream	크림	[keu-rim]

ENGLISH LOANWORDS: FOOD

dessert	디저트	[di-jeo-teu]
doughnut	도넛	[do-neot]
ham	햄	[haem]
hamburger	햄버거	[haem-beo-geo]
ice cream	아이스크림	[a-i-seu-keu-rim]
jam	잼	[jaem]
jelly	젤리	[jel-li]
juice	주스	[ju-seu]
ketchup	케챂	[ke-chap]
meat ball	미트볼	[mi-teu-bol]
milk shake	밀크쉐이크	[mil-keu-shye-i-keu]
muffin	머핀	[meo-pin]

(N) pie 파이 [pa-i]

(N) pudding 푸딩 [pu-ding]

(N) roll 롤 [rol]

(N) salad 샐러드 [sael-leo-deu]

(N) sandwich 샌드위치 [saen-deu-wi-chi]

(N) slush 슬러시 [seul-leo-shi]

(N) soup 수프 [su-peu]

(N) steak 스테이크 [seu-te-i-keu]

(N) toast 토스트 [to-seu-teu]

(N) waffle 와플 [wa-peul]

(N) yogurt 요거트 [yo-geo-teu]

(N) avocado	아보카도	[a-bo-ka-do]
(N) banana	바나나	[ba-na-na]
(N) blueberry	블루베리	[beul-lu-be-ri]
(N) cherry	체리	[che-ri]
(N) coconut	코코넛	[ko-ko-neot]
(N) guava	구아바	[gu-a-ba]
(N) kiwi	키위	[ki-wi]
(N) lemon	레몬	[le-mon]
(N) mango	망고	[man-go]
(N) melon	멜론	[mel-lon]
(N) orange	오렌지	[o-ren-ji]
(N) papaya	파파야	[pa-pa-ya]

ENGLISH LOANWORDS: FRUITS

(N) pineapple	파인애플	[pa-i-nae-peul]
(N) tomato	토마토	[to-ma-to]

ENGLISH LOANWORDS: VEGETABLES

(N) aloe	알로에	[al-lo-e]
(N) broccoli	브로콜리	[beu-ro-kol-li]
(N) celery	셀러리	[sel-leo-ri]
(N) olive	올리브	[ol-li-beu]
(N) paprika, bell pepper	파프리카	[pa-peu-ri-ka]
(N) parsley	파슬리	[pa-seul-li]

(N)	apartment	아파트	[a-pa-teu]
(N)	building	빌딩	[bil-ding]
(N)	carpet	카펫	[ka-pet]
(N)	container	컨테이너	[keon-te-i-neo]
(N)	cup	컵	[keop]
(N)	curtain	커튼	[keo-teun]
(N)	elevator	엘레베이터	[el-le-be-i-teo]
(N)	fork	포크	[po-keu]
(N)	frying-pan	후라이팬	[hu-ra-i-paen]
(N)	gas range	가스렌지	[ga-seu-ren-ji]
(N)	hotel	호텔	[ho-tel]
(N)	kitchen towel	키친타월	[ki-chin-ta-wol]

ENGLISH LOANWORDS: HOME

(N) lamp	램프	[laem-peu]
(N) mixer	믹서기	[mig-seo-gi]
(N) oven	오븐	[o-beun]
(N) shower	샤워	[sha-wo]
(N) sofa	소파	[so-pa]
(N) sponge	스폰지	[seu-pon-ji]
(N) standing lamp	스탠드	[seu-taen-deu]
(N) table	테이블	[te-i-beul]

ENGLISH LOANWORDS: ENTERTAINMENT

| (N) game | 게임 | [ge-im] |
| (N) puzzle | 퍼즐 | [peo-jeul] |

ENGLISH LOANWORDS: MUSIC

(N) bass	베이스	[be-i-seu]
(N) cello	첼로	[chel-lo]
(N) classic	클래식	[keul-lae-shig]
(N) concert	콘서트	[kon-seo-teu]
(N) drum	드럼	[deu-reom]
(N) flute	플룻	[peul-lut]
(N) guitar	기타	[gi-ta]
(N) jazz	재즈	[jae-jeu]
(N) piano	피아노	[pi-a-no]
(N) rock	락	[rag]
(N) trumpet	트럼펫	[teu-reom-pet]
(N) violin	바이올린	[ba-i-ol-lin]

belly-dance	벨리댄스	[bel-li-daen-seu]
fencing	펜싱	[pen-shing]
figure-skate	피겨	[pi-gyeo]
golf	골프	[gol-peu]
hockey	하키	[ha-ki]
jogging	조깅	[jo-ging]
racing	레이싱	[re-i-shing]
racket ball	라켓볼	[ra-ket-bol]
skate	스케이트	[seu-ke-i-teu]
ski	스키	[seu-ki]
squash	스쿼시	[seu-kwo-shi]
tennis	테니스	[te-ni-seu]

ENGLISH LOANWORDS: JOBS

artist   아티스트   [a-ti-seu-teu]

ballerina   발레리나   [bal-le-ri-na]

chef   셰프   [shye-peu]

coach   코치   [ko-chi]

columnist   칼럼니스트   [kal-leom-ni-seu-teu]

designer   디자이너   [di-ja-i-neo]

manager   매니저   [mae-ni-jeo]

model   모델   [mo-del]

musician   뮤지션   [myu-ji-shyeon]

programmer   프로그래머   [peu-ro-geu-rae-meo]

staff   스태프   [seu-tae-peu]

stewardess   스튜어디스   [seu-tyu-eo-di-seu]

battery	배터리	[bae-teo-ri]
camera	카메라	[ka-me-ra]
computer	컴퓨터	[keom-pyu-teo]
e-mail	이메일	[i-me-il]
notebook	노트북	[no-teu-bug]
pastel	파스텔	[pa-seu-tel]
pen	펜	[pen]
portfolio	포트폴리오	[po-teu-pol-li-o]
radio	라디오	[ra-di-o]
remote control	리모컨	[ri-mo-keon]
tape	테이프	[te-i-peu]
television	텔레비전	[tel-le-bi-jeon]

(N) accelerator	악셀	[ag-sel]
(N) boat	보트	[bo-teu]
(N) brake	브레이크	[beu-re-i-keu]
(N) bus	버스	[beo-seu]
(N) motorcycle	오토바이	[o-to-ba-i]
(N) pedal	페달	[pe-dal]
(N) taxi	택시	[taeg-shi]
(N) terminal	터미널	[teo-mi-neol]
(N) truck	트럭	[teu-reog]

(2) LOANWORDS FROM OTHER LANGUAGES

Historically, Chinese was the biggest influence on the Korean vocabulary. Ancient Chinese words are mostly used as prefixes or suffixes to compose words - which are quite different from modern Chinese words. Although we present prefixes and suffixes originating from Chinese in Chapter 12, we list below some Chinese-based loanwords that have similar pronunciations with modern Chinese.

CHINESE LOANWORDS

(N) cartoon 만화 [man-hwa]

(N) cheers 건배 [keon-bae]

(N) China 중국 [jung-gug]

(N) dragon 용 [yong]

(N) mountain 산 [san]

(N) tea 차 [cha]

(N) tofu 두부 [du-bu]

(N) tradition 전통 [jeon-tong]

On the other hand, loanwords from Japanese and European languages (except English) predominantly describe food items.

JAPANESE LOANWORDS

ⓝ ramen	라면	[ra-myeon]
ⓝ udon noodle	우동	[u-dong]
ⓝ wasabi	와사비	[wa-sa-bi]

ITALIAN LOANWORDS

ⓝ cafe latte	카페라떼	[ka-pe-ra-dde]
ⓝ lasagna	라자냐	[ra-ja-nya]
ⓝ pasta	파스타	[pa-seu-ta]
ⓝ pizza	피자	[pi-ja]
ⓝ spaghetti	스파게티	[seu-pa-ge-ti]

FRENCH LOANWORDS

(N) baguette   바게트   [ba-ge-teu]

(N) bell pepper   피망   [pi-mang]
(French: piment)

(N) buffet   부페   [bu-pe]

(N) camambert   까망베르   [gga-mang-be-reu]

(N) champagne   샴페인   [shyam-pe-in]

(N) crepes   크레페   [keu-re-pe]

(N) croissant   크루아상   [keu-ru-a-sang]

(N) mousse   무스   [mu-seu]

(N) sorbet   샤베트   [shya-be-teu]

OTHER

(N) harmonika (German) 하모니카 [ha-mo-ni-ka]

(N) nacho (Spanish) 나초 [na-cho]

(N) part-time job 아르바이트 [a-reu-ba-i-teu]
(German: Arbeit, lit. work)

(N) salsa (Spanish) 살사 [sal-sa]

(N) tobacco (Portuguese) 담배 [dam-be]

(N) yoga (Indian) 요가 [yo-ga]

(3) COUNTRY NAMES

Most country names used in Korean can be considered as loanwords, as they are directly adopted from their original name and written in Hangeul. We list some common country names below.

Austria 오스트리아 [o-seu-teu-ri-a]

Belgium 벨기에 [bel-gi-e]

Brazil 브라질 [beu-ra-jil]

Cambodia 캄보디아 [kam-bo-di-a]

Canada 캐나다 [kae-na-da]

Costa Rica 코스타리카 [ko-seu-ta-ri-ka]

Cuba 쿠바 [ku-ba]

Czech 체코 [che-ko]

Denmark 덴마크 [den-ma-keu]

Egypt 이집트 [i-jip-teu]

Finland 핀란드 [pil-lan-deu]PR3.6

France 프랑스 [peu-rang-seu]

(N) Greece   그리스   [geu-ri-seu]

(N) Hong Kong   홍콩   [hong-kong]

(N) Hungary   헝가리   [heong-ga-ri]

(N) India   인도   [in-do]

(N) Indonesia   인도네시아   [in-do-ne-shi-a]

(N) Iran   이란   [i-ran]

(N) Iraq   이라크   [i-ra-keu]

(N) Israel   이스라엘   [i-seu-ra-el]

(N) Italy   이태리   [i-tae-ri]

(N) Jamaica   자메이카   [ja-me-i-ka]

(N) Kazakhstan   카자흐스탄   [ka-ja-heu-seu-tan]

(N) Kenya   케냐   [ke-nya]

Libya 리비아 [ri-bi-a]

Malaysia 말레이시아 [mal-le-i-shi-a]

Mexico 멕시코 [meg-shi-ko]

Mongolia 몽골 [mong-gol]

Myanmar 미얀마 [mi-yan-ma]

Nepal 네팔 [ne-pal]

Netherlands 네덜란드 [ne-deol-lan-deu]

Norway 노르웨이 [no-reu-we-i]

Pakistan 파키스탄 [pa-ki-seu-tan]

Peru 페루 [pe-ru]

Philippines 필리핀 [pil-li-pin]

Poland 폴란드 [pol-lan-deu]

(N) Portugal   포르투갈   [po-reu-tu-gal]

(N) Russia   러시아   [reo-shi-a]

(N) Scotland   스코트랜드   [seu-ko-teu-raen-deu]

(N) Singapore   싱가폴   [shing-ga-pol]

(N) Spain   스페인   [seu-pe-in]

(N) Sweden   스웨덴   [seu-we-den]

(N) Switzerland   스위스   [seu-wi-seu]

(N) Turkey   터키   [teo-ki]

(N) Uganda   우간다   [u-gan-da]

(N) Ukraine   우크라이나   [u-keu-ra-i-na]

(N) Uzbekistan   우즈베키스탄   [u-jeu-be-ki-seu-tan]

(N) Vietnam   베트남   [be-teu-nam]

The countries for which their Korean name is different from their English name are listed below.

COUNTRY NAMES

Australia	호주	[ho-ju]
China	중국	[jung-gug]
England	영국	[yeong-gug]
Germany	독일	[do-gil]PR1.1
Japan	일본	[il-bon]
Korea	한국	[han-gug]
South Africa	남아프리카 공화국	[na-ma-peu-ri-ka-gong-hwa-gug]
Thailand	태국	[tae-gug]
USA	미국	[mi-gug]

To make a word that refers to the people living in the country, put the word '사람[sa-ram]' after the nationality in casual contexts:

한국		사람		한국사람
[han-gug]	+	[sa-ram]	➡	[han-gug-sa-ram]
Korea		person		Korean

Or, you can put a Sino-Korean suffix '인[in]' after the nationality in formal contexts:

한국		인		한국인
[han-gug]	+	[in]	➡	[han-gu-gin] [PR1.1]
Korea		person		Korean

To make a word that means the language spoken in the country, put a Sino-Korean suffix '어[eo]' after the nationality.

한국   +   어   ➡   한국어

[han-gug]   [eo]   [han-gu-geo] PR1.1

Korea   language   Korean language

You can also add '말[mal]' to make a language name. However, not all languages can be combined with mal, such as English.

한국   +   말   ➡   한국말

[han-gug]   [mal]   [han-gung-mal] PR3.1

Korea   language   Korean language

EXAMPLES

영어[yeong-eo]: English language

프랑스어[peu-rang-seu-eo]: French language

스페인어[seu-pe-i-neo] PR1.1: Spanish language

외국어[we-gu-geo] PR1.1: Foreign Language

미국사람[mi-gug-sa-ram]: American

독일인[do-gi-rin]PR1.1: German

We are social animals.
Our lives are enriched through
interactions with other people.
We enjoy talking with others
how things are going.
Accordingly, learning vocabulary
about the human body, feelings
and emotions will boost your
ability to connect with Koreans.

HUMAN

(1) CHARACTERISTICS

나 [na] : I

너 [neo] : you

I say "NOW!"

You say "NO!"

Starting from this chapter, we will provide some associations as memory aid. For example, the Korean word for 'I' is '나[na].' Draw an image in your imagination of yourself saying 'now.' In that way, you can make a connection between the word 'I' and '나[na].' Ideally, you can create a logical connection between yourself and why you say "now" when you are looking for the word "I", so that you remember "I say now" when you think of yourself. Create a vivid image in your mind with this association and you will be surprised how quickly you can remember the word. For more information about association-based learning please refer to Pages 18-20.

인간 [in-gan] : human
There's a human IN GONdola.

이름 [i-reum] : name
How do you pronounce my name in IRAN?

성 [seong] : family name, gender
She sang a SONG about her family name.

소녀 [so-nyeo] : girl
SONYA is a girl.

나이 [na-i] : age
He was a bit NAIve for his age.

죽다 [jug-dda]PR1.3 : to die

The man died
from eating
too much SUGar.[7]

살다 [sal-da] : to live
The woman makes a living
by selling SALt.

---

7 In case of verbs, we create an association only for
the verb stem, without "다".

(N) adult	어른	[eo-reun]
(N) age	나이	[na-i]
(N) baby	아기	[a-gi]
(N) boy	소년	[so-nyeon]
(N) child	아이	[a-i]
(N) citizen	국민	[gung-min]PR3.1
(N) country	나라	[na-ra]
(N) elderly	노인	[no-in]
(N) ethnic group	민족	[min-jog]
(N) family name, gender	성	[seong]
(N) female	여성	[yeo-seong]
(N) girl	소녀	[so-nyeo]

N human	인간	[in-gan]
N I	나	[na]
N individual	개인	[gae-in]
N male	남성	[nam-seong]
N man	남자	[nam-ja]
N name	이름	[i-reum]
N nation	국가	[gug-gga]PR1.3
N oneself	자신	[ja-shin]
N person	사람	[sa-ram]
N teenager	청소년	[cheong-so-nyeon]
N woman	여자	[yeo-ja]
N you	너	[neo]

(N) youngster 어린이 [eo-ri-ni]PR1.1

(N) youth 청년 [cheong-nyeon]

(Aj) old 늙다 [neug-dda]PR2.2 PR1.3

(Aj) young 어리다 [eo-ri-da]

(Aj) youthful 젊다 [jeom-dda]PR2.2 PR1.3

(V) to become 되다 [dwe-da]

(V) to call 부르다 [bu-reu-da]

(V) to die 죽다 [jug-dda]PR1.3

(V) to kill 죽이다 [ju-gi-da]PR1.1

(V) to live 살다 [sal-da]

(V) to save (a person) 살리다 [sal-li-da]

EXERCISE

나라 1		a oneself
죽다 2		b to become
민족 3		c to live
어른 4		d to die
성 5		e old
살다 6		f adult
자신 7		g family name
부르다 8		h ethnic group
늙다 9		i country
되다 10		j to call

1-i, 2-d, 3-h, 4-f, 5-g, 6-c, 7-a, 8-j, 9-e, 10-b

나이 is _____ in English.

나라 is _____ in English.

어리다 is _____ in English.

A name is _____ in Korean.

A person is _____ in Korean.

A woman is _____ in Korean.

The boy becomes an adult :

소년(Subject)이 어른이 되다(Verb).

*The word order in Korean is quite different from other western languages. We can see, for example, the object comes first and the verb comes later. Don't worry if you have no idea at this stage! We'll study these aspects in the next two books.

A young man : 어린 _____

The girl calls the baby : _____ 가 아기를_____ .

age, country, young, 이름, 사람, 여자,
남자. 소녀, 부르다.

(2) BODY

몸 [mom] : body
MOM made my body.

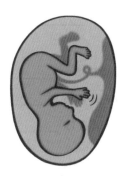

배 [bae] : belly
My belly looks like a BAgel.

등 [deung] : back
What are you DOING behind my back?

목 [mog] : neck
MOKaccino is flowing down my neck.

땀 [ddam] : sweat
A DAM is holding back a lake full of sweat.

어깨 [eo-ggae] : shoulder
My shoulders are OK.

귀 [gwi] : ear
Listen to the GUItar
with your ears.

엉덩이 [eong-deong-i] : buttock
A butterfly is sitting
ON DONKEY's buttock.

손 [son] : hand
Give me your hand, SON.

발 [bal] : foot
Kick the BALL with your foot.

무릎 [mu-reup] : knee
A cow is hurting its knee
doing the MOO-RAP.

눈 [nun] : eye
Eyes are usually open at NOON.

코 [ko] : nose
KOala has a big nose.

턱 [teog] : Chin
We move our chins when we TALK.

얼굴 [eol-gul] : face
Her face was covered with ALL GOLd.

팔 [pal] : arm
He puts his arm on my shoulder and said,
'Hey PAL!'

다리 [da-ri] : leg
TERRY has long legs.

감다 [gam-dda]PR1.3 : to wash (hair)
COME wash your hair!

집다 [jip-dda]PR1.3 : to pick
I'd like to pick up some CHIPs.

떨다 [ddeol-da] : to tremble
The queen was trembling when the needle was stuck into the voodoo DOLL.

하다 [ha-da] : to do
HAha! I can do anything.

말다 [mal-da] : to stop
Stop being MALicious.

흘리다 [heul-li-da] : to shed, to bleed
The HOOLIgan bleed from a fight with the fans of the other team.

HUMAN: BODY

ⓝ ankle	발목	[bal-mog]
ⓝ arm	팔	[pal]
ⓝ back	등	[deung]
ⓝ belly	배	[bae]
ⓝ belly button	배꼽	[bae-ggop]
ⓝ blood	피	[pi]
ⓝ body	몸	[mom]
ⓝ bone	뼈	[bbyeo]
ⓝ buttock	엉덩이	[eong-deong-i]
ⓝ cheek	뺨	[bbyam]
ⓝ chest/breast	가슴	[ga-seum]
ⓝ chin	턱	[teog]

HUMAN: BODY

(N) ear 귀 [gwi]

(N) elbow 팔꿈치 [pal-ggum-chi]

(N) eye 눈 [nun]

(N) eyebrow 눈썹 [nun-sseop]

(N) face 얼굴 [eol-gul]

(N) finger 손가락 [son-gga-rag]PR1.3

(N) fingernail 손톱 [son-top]

(N) flesh 살 [sal]

(N) foot 발 [bal]

(N) forehead 이마 [i-ma]

(N) fur (body hair) 털 [teol]

(N) hair 머리카락 [meo-ri-ka-rag]

N			
hand	손	[son]	
head	머리	[meo-ri]	
height (body)	키	[ki]	
height (object)	높이	[no-pi] PR1.1	
knee	무릎	[mu-reup]	
leg	다리	[da-ri]	
lip	입술	[ip-sul]	
mouth	입	[ip]	
muscle	근육	[geu-nyug] PR1.1	
lower head including neck	고개	[go-gae]	
neck	목	[mog]	
nose	코	[ko]	

N			
shoulder	어깨	[eo-ggae]	
skin	피부	[pi-bu]	
sweat	땀	[ddam]	
tear	눈물	[nun-mul]	
toe	발가락	[bal-gga-rag]	PR1.3
toenail	발톱	[bal-top]	
tongue	혀	[hyeo]	
tooth	이/이빨	[i] / [i-bbal]	
voice	목소리	[mog-sso-ri]	PR1.3
weight	무게	[mu-ge]	
whole body	온몸	[on-mom]	
wrist	손목	[son-mog]	

HUMAN: BODY

(v) to wear (on fingers)   끼다   [ggi-da]

(v) to do   하다   [ha-da]

(v) not to do   앉다   [an-ta] PR4.1

(v) to pick   집다   [jip-dda] PR1.3

(v) to shed (tears), to bleed 흘리다 [heul-li-da]

(v) to stop   말다   [mal-da]

(v) to tremble   떨다   [ddeol-da]

(v) to wash (hair)   감다   [gam-dda] PR1.3

EXERCISE

등	1	a	bone
피부	2	b	back
뼈	3	c	blood
근육	4	d	skin
피	5	e	flesh
살	6	f	height
키	7	g	muscle
무게	8	h	weight
머리	9	i	neck
목	10	j	head

1-b, 2-d, 3-a, 4-g, 5-c, 6-e, 7-f, 8-h, 9-j, 10-i

배꼽 is _____ in English.

다리 is _____ in English.

귀 is _____ in English.

Hand is _____ in Korean.

Foot is _____ in Korean.

Nose is _____ in Korean.

I wash my hair. : 나는 _____ 를 _____ .

Shake body. : _____ 을 _____ .

Shed tears. : _____ 을 _____ .

belly button, legs, ears, 손, 발, 코, 머리 감다, 몸 흔들다, 눈물 흘리다

(3) FEELINGS & EMOTIONS

미소 [mi-so] : smile
She had a big smile while having a bowl of MISO soup.

소리 [so-ri] : sound
Oops! SORRY for that sound.

맛 [mat] : taste
I tasted a MAT. Yuck!

말 [mal] : talk
At the MALL is a good place to talk.

재미 [jae-mi] : fun
JAM-EATing is fun.

미움 [mi-um] : dislike
You dislike ME? UMM..

고민 [go-min] : worry
COME IN and tell me your worries.

나쁘다 [na-bbeu-da] : bad
It's bad to take a NAP ON the wheel.

달다 [dal-da] : sweet
Too much sweet food makes my tongue DULL.

쓰다 [sseu-da] : bitter
Life is bitter SWEEt.

맵다 [maep-dda] PR1.3 : spicy
We dropped some spices on the MAP.

짜다 [jja-da] : salty
CHArlie's angels like salty crackers.

보다 [bo-da] : to see
I see the BOAT.

맡다 [mat-dda] PR1.3 : to smell
You smell the stinky yoga MAT.

만지다 [man-ji-da] : to touch
Don't touch it, MAN. It's a CHEETAH!

놀라다 [nol-la-da] : to be surprised
I was surprised that I saw NO LAnd.

숨다 [sum-dda]PR1.3 : to hide
I hide SOME of my gifts.

원하다 [won-ha-da] : to want
I only WANt one house.

N affection	정	[jeong]
N behavior	행동	[haeng-dong]
N breath	숨	[sum]
N crying	울음	[u-reum] PR1.1
N despair	절망	[jeol-mang]
N disappointment	실망	[shil-mang]
N displeasure	미움	[mi-um]
N dissatisfaction	불만	[bul-man]
N emotion	감정	[gam-jeong]
N expression	표현	[pyo-hyeon]
N facial expression	표정	[pyo-jeong]
N feeling	느낌	[neu-ggim]

fragrance	향기	[hyang-gi]
fun	재미	[jae-mi]
gaze / look	시선	[shi-sun]
happiness	행복	[haeng-bog]
hatred	증오	[jeung-o]
hope	희망	[hee-mang]
interest	관심	[gwan-shim]
joy	즐거움	[jeul-geo-um]
laughter	웃음	[u-seum]
love	사랑	[sa-rang]
memory	기억	[ki-eog]
mind	마음	[ma-eum]

N			
mood	기분	[ki-bun]
pain	고통	[go-tong]
pleasure	기쁨	[ki-bbeum]
rage	분노	[bun-no]
sadness	슬픔	[seul-peum]
satisfaction	만족	[man-jog]
sense	감각	[gam-gag]
smell, odor	냄새	[naem-sae]
smile	미소	[mi-so]
song	노래	[no-rae]
sound	소리	[so-ri]
talk	말	[mal]

(N) taste 맛 [mat]

(N) tension (nervous) 긴장 [kin-jang]

(N) wits, sense 눈치 [nun-chi]

(N) worry 고민 [go-min]

(N) worry 걱정 [geog-jjeong] PR1.3

(Aj) bad 나쁘다 [na-bbeu-da]

(Aj) bitter 쓰다 [sseu-da]

(Aj) dislike 싫다 [shil-ta] PR4.1

(Aj) good 좋다 [jo-ta] PR4.1

(Aj) happy 기쁘다 [gi-bbeu-da]

(Aj) hot, spicy 맵다 [maep-dda] PR1.3

(Aj) sad 슬프다 [seul-peu-da]

HUMAN: FEELINGS & EMOTIONS

Aj salty 짜다 [jja-da]

Aj scary, scared 무섭다 [mu-seop-dda] PR1.3

Aj strange 이상하다 [i-sang-ha-da]

Aj sweet 달다 [dal-da]

V to be located 놓이다 [no-i-da] PR5

V to be surprised 놀라다 [nol-la-da]

V to breathe 숨쉬다 [sum-shwi-da]

V to hear 듣다 [deut-dda] PR1.3

V to be heard 들리다 [deul-li-da]

V to hide 숨다 [sum-dda] PR1.3

V to like 좋아하다 [jo-a-ha-da] PR5

V to see 보다 [bo-da]

(v) to be seen 보이다 [bo-i-da]

(v) to smell 맡다 [mat-dda] PR1.3

(v) to taste 맛보다 [mat-bo-da]

(v) to touch 만지다 [man-ji-da]

(v) to want 원하다 [won-ha-da]

(v) to wish 바라다 [ba-ra-da]

EXERCISE

소리 **1**	**a** bad
냄새 **2**	**b** sound
나쁘다 **3**	**c** happy
기쁘다 **4**	**d** to wish
이상하다 **5**	**e** to hear
보다 **6**	**f** to like
듣다 **7**	**g** smell
좋아하다 **8**	**h** strange
원하다 **9**	**i** to see
바라다 **10**	**j** to want

1-b, 2-g, 3-a, 4-c, 5-h, 6-i, 7-e, 8-f, 9-j, 10-d

마음 is _____ in English.

기억 is _____ in English.

걱정 is _____ in English.

Mood is _____ in Korean.

Love is _____ in Korean.

To be good is _____ in Korean.

A bitter taste : 쓴 _____

The sound is heard : _____가 들리다.

To see the hope : _____을 _____.

mind, memory, worry, 기분, 사랑, 좋다, 맛, 소리, 희망, 보다.

The extensive vocabulary to describe family relationships is an indication of the central importance of family in Korean society. Any person you meet is believed to be part of an extensive family and thus denoted with a family name: a waitress is 이모, a woman's older male friend is 오빠, a male's older female friend is 누나. Koreans are one big happy family!

FAMILY

(1) SIBLINGS

Family is an important matter in Korean society. This fact is reflected in the language itself, so family-related terms are widely developed in the family-oriented society.

One interesting cultural fact is that everyone is considered as a family member. Aside your friends who can be your brothers and sisters, you will see a shopper calling a vendor '언니[eon-ni]: older sister.' You may also hear people in a restaurant call a waitress '이모[i-mo] aunt, mother side.'

Another fact is that the family terms for older generations are more detailed than the terms for younger generations. Also, the speaker's gender is an important factor to decide what term should be used among siblings.

· For male speakers:

형 [hyeong] : older brother
The older brother is feeling too YOUNG.

누나 [nu-na] : older sister
When my big sister is on a diet, she always eats
TUNA for dinner.

· For female speakers:

오빠 [o-bba] : older brother
OBBA Gangnam style!

언니 [eon-ni] : older sister
ONLY me and my big sister are left at home.

• For both male and female speakers:

동생 [dong-saeng] : younger sibling

I said to my younger brother and sister, "DON'T SAY anything about what you saw!"

FAMILY: SIBLINGS

older brother	형 오빠	[hyeong] [o-bba]
older sister	누나 언니	[nu-na] [eon-ni]
younger sibling	동생	[dong-saeng]

(2) PARENTS, CHILDREN, AND RELATIVES

어머니

[eo-meo-ni] : mother

My mother said,
"OH, MONEY!"

아버지 [a-beo-ji] : father

My father said, "AH, BUSY..."

엄마 [eom-ma] : mom
UMM, MOm?

아들 [a-deul] : son
My son is an ADULt.

딸 [ddal] : daughter
My daughter has a DOLL face.

가족 [ga-jog] : family
My family CAN JOKE about it.

아내 [a-nae] : wife
I have A NEW wife.

부인 [bu-in] : wife, madam
My wife said BOO IN the Halloween party.

친척 [chin-cheog] : relative
Because of my funny chin, my relatives always
make a CHIN JOKE.

115

(N)	dad	아빠	[a-bba]
(N)	daughter	딸	[ddal]
(N)	family	가족	[ga-jog]
(N)	father	아버지	[a-beo-ji]
(N)	grand daughter	손녀	[son-nyeo]
(N)	grand son	손자	[son-ja]
(N)	grandfather	할아버지	[ha-ra-beo-ji] PR1.1
(N)	grandmother	할머니	[hal-meo-ni]
(N)	honey, darling	여보	[yeo-bo]
(N)	husband	남편	[nam-pyeon]
(N)	husband & wife	부부	[bu-bu]
(N)	marriage	결혼	[gyeol-hon]

FAMILY: PARENTS & CHILDREN

(N) mom   엄마   [eom-ma]

(N) mother   어머니   [eo-meo-ni]

(N) offspring   자녀   [ja-nyeo]

(N) parents   부모   [bu-mo]

(N) son   아들   [a-deul]

(N) spouse   배우자   [bae-u-ja]

(N) wife   아내   [a-nae]

(N) wife, madam   부인   [bu-in]

FAMILY: RELATIVES

Ⓝ aunt (dad's sister)	고모	[go-mo]
Ⓝ aunt (mom's sister)	이모	[i-mo]
Ⓝ aunt (uncle's wife)	숙모	[sung-mo]PR3.1
Ⓝ aunt / ma'am	아주머니	[a-ju-meo-ni]
Ⓝ aunt / ma'am	아줌마	[a-jum-ma]
Ⓝ cousin	사촌	[sa-chon]
Ⓝ daughter's husband	사위	[sa-wi]
Ⓝ house, family	댁	[daeg]
Ⓝ husband's father	시아버지	[shi-a-beo-ji]
Ⓝ husband's mother	시어머니	[shi-eo-meo-ni]
Ⓝ niece	조카	[jo-ka]
Ⓝ older brother's wife	형수	[hyeong-su]

FAMILY: RELATIVES

(N) relatives	친척	[chin-cheog]
(N) son's wife	며느리	[myeo-neu-ri]
(N) uncle	삼촌	[sam-chon]
(N) uncle / mister	아저씨	[a-jeo-ssi]
(N) wife's father	장인	[jang-in]
(N) wife's mother	장모	[jang-mo]
(N) younger brother's wife	제수	[je-su]
(V) to have	가지다	[ga-ji-da]
(V) to help	돕다	[dop-dda] PR1.3
(V) to take care of	모시다	[mo-shi-da]

For more advanced learners, we show the terms of a family tree from different perspectives. Page 121 shows the two family trees from the perspective of a male or female child. Page 122 shows the larger tree of aunts and uncles again from a child's perspective.

male
female
male or female

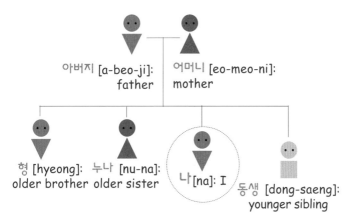

아버지 [a-beo-ji]: father
어머니 [eo-meo-ni]: mother
형 [hyeong]: older brother
누나 [nu-na]: older sister
나[na]: I
동생 [dong-saeng]: younger sibling

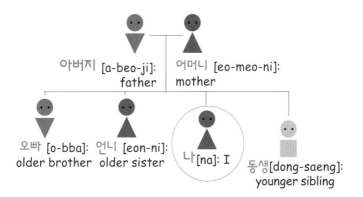

아버지 [a-beo-ji]: father
어머니 [eo-meo-ni]: mother
오빠 [o-bba]: older brother
언니 [eon-ni]: older sister
나[na]: I
동생[dong-saeng]: younger sibling

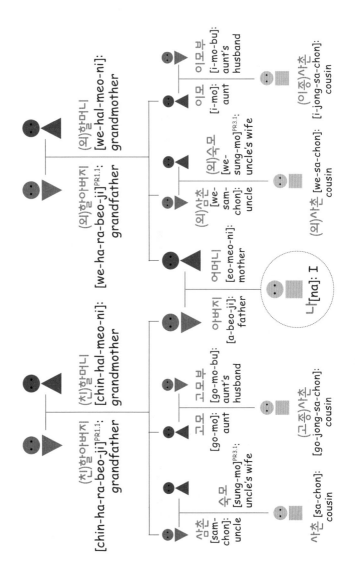

(친)할아버지[PR1.1] [chin-ha-ra-beo-ji]: grandfather

(친)할머니 [chin-hal-meo-ni]: grandmother

(외)할아버지[PR1.1] [we-ha-ra-beo-ji]: grandfather

(외)할머니 [we-hal-meo-ni]: grandmother

삼촌 [sam-chon]: uncle

숙모 [sung-mo][PR3.1]: uncle's wife

고모 [go-mo]: aunt

고모부 [go-mo-bu]: aunt's husband

아버지 [a-beo-ji]: father

어머니 [eo-meo-ni]: mother

(외)삼촌 [we-sam-chon]: uncle

(외)숙모 [we-sung-mo][PR3.1]: uncle's wife

이모 [i-mo]: aunt

이모부 [i-mo-bu]: aunt's husband

사촌 [sa-chon]: cousin

(고종)사촌 [go-jong-sa-chon]: cousin

나 [na]: I

(외)사촌 [we-sa-chon]: cousin

(이종)사촌 [i-jong-sa-chon]: cousin

The following pages show the family trees for a husband and wife. Knowledge of these trees can help you handle your family relations with a smile if you are married in a Korean family!

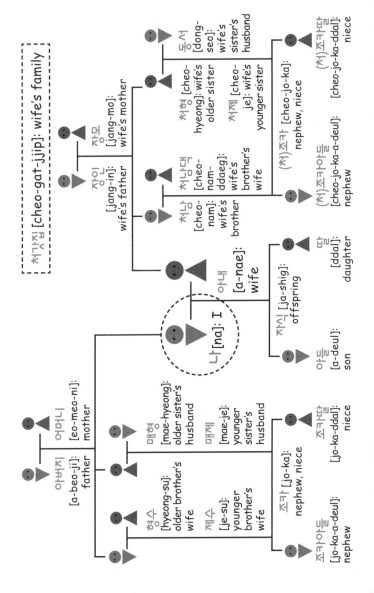

처갓집 [cheo-gat-jjip]: wife's family

처모 [jang-mo]: wife's mother
장인 [jang-in]: wife's father

동서 [dong-seo]: wife's sister's husband
처형 [cheo-hyeong]: wife's older sister
처제 [cheo-je]: wife's younger sister
처남댁 [cheo-nam-ddaeg]: wife's brother's wife
처남 [cheo-nam]: wife's brother

(처)조카딸 [cheo-jo-ka-ddal]: niece
(처)조카 [cheo-jo-ka]: nephew, niece
(처)조카아들 [cheo-jo-ka-a-deul]: nephew

아내 [a-nae]: wife
나 [na]: I
자식 [ja-shig]: offspring
딸 [ddal]: daughter
아들 [a-deul]: son

어머니 [eo-meo-ni]: mother
아버지 [a-beo-ji]: father
매형 [mae-hyeong]: older sister's husband
매제 [mae-je]: younger sister's husband
형수 [hyeong-su]: older brother's wife
제수 [je-su]: younger brother's wife

조카 [jo-ka]: nephew, niece
조카딸 [jo-ka-ddal]: niece
조카아들 [jo-ka-a-deul]: nephew

124

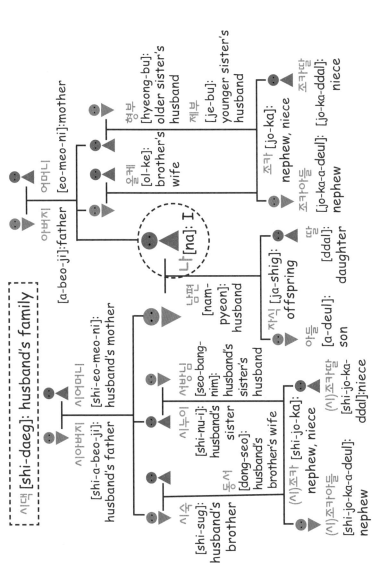

시댁 [shi-daeg]: husband's family

아버지 [a-beo-ji]:father
어머니 [eo-meo-ni]:mother

나 [na]: I

형부 [hyeong-bu]: older sister's husband
제부 [je-bu]: younger sister's husband

올케 [ol-ke]: brother's wife

조카 [jo-ka]: nephew, niece
조카아들 [jo-ka-a-deul]: nephew
조카딸 [jo-ka-ddal]: niece

남편 [nam-pyeon]: husband
자식 [ja-shig]: offspring
딸 [ddal]: daughter
아들 [a-deul]: son

시아버지 [shi-a-beo-ji]: husband's father
시어머니 [shi-eo-meo-ni]: husband's mother

서방님 [seo-bang-nim]: husband's sister's husband
시누이 [shi-nu-i]: husband's sister
동서 [dong-seo]: husband's brother's wife
시숙 [shi-sug]: husband's brother

(시)조카 [shi-jo-ka]: nephew, niece
(시)조카딸 [shi-jo-ka-ddal]:niece
(시)조카아들 [shi-jo-ka-a-deul]: nephew

125

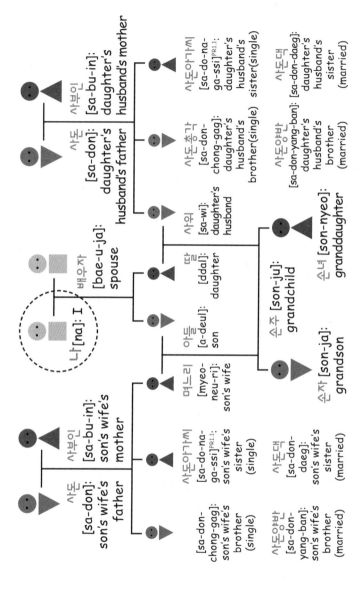

사부인 [sa-bu-in]: daughter's husband's mother

사돈 [sa-don]: daughter's husband's father

사돈아가씨 [sa-do-na-ga-ssi]^{PR1.1}: daughter's husband's sister(single)

사돈총각 [sa-don-chong-gag]: daughter's husband's brother(single)

사돈댁 [sa-don-daeg]: daughter's husband's sister (married)

사돈양반 [sa-don-yang-ban]: daughter's husband's brother (married)

사위 [sa-wi]: daughter's husband

배우자 [bae-u-ja]: spouse

나 [na]: I

딸 [ddal]: daughter

아들 [a-deul]: son

손주 [son-ju]: grandchild

손녀 [son-nyeo]: granddaughter

손자 [son-ja]: grandson

며느리 [myeo-neu-ri]: son's wife

사부인 [sa-bu-in]: son's wife's mother

사돈 [sa-don]: son's wife's father

사돈아가씨 [sa-do-na-ga-ssi]^{PR1.1}: son's wife's sister (single)

사돈댁 [sa-don-daeg]: son's wife's sister (married)

[sa-don-chong-gag]: son's wife's brother (single)

사돈양반 [sa-don-yang-ban]: son's wife's brother (married)

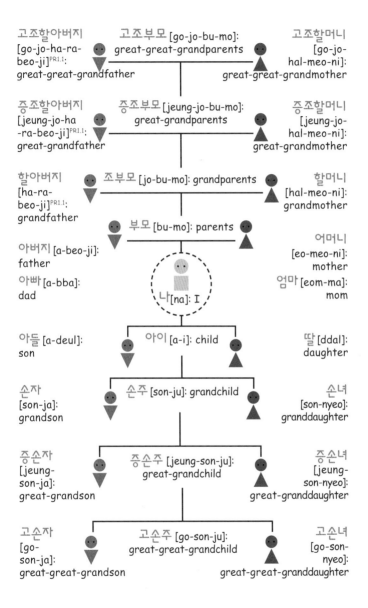

EXERCISE

동생 1   a grandfather

할머니 2   b aunt/ma'am

할아버지 3   c parents

아들 4   d daughter

딸 5   e grandmother

부모 6   f wife/madam

부인 7   g younger sibling

오빠 8   h uncle/mister

아저씨 9   i older brother

아주머니 10   j son

1-g, 2-e, 3-a, 4-j, 5-d, 6-c, 7-f, 8-i, 9-h, 10-b

이모 is _____ in English.

가족 is _____ in English.

결혼 is _____ in English.

Mom is _____ in Korean.

A wife is _____ in Korean.

An older sister from a girl is _____ in Korean.

The grandmother helps the older brother (from a boy). :

_____ 가 _____ 을 _____ .

The son takes care of the parents. :

_____이 _____ 를 _____ .

The uncle(mister) has a daughter. :

_____ 가 _____ 을 _____ .

aunt, family, marriage, 엄마, 아내(부인), 언니, 할머니, 형, 돕다, 아들, 부모, 모시다, 아저씨. 딸, 가지다.

Every morning we begin our life by going to a place. Wherever we travel, it is important to find the destination. This chapter introduces the words related to public places we visit frequently in our daily life such as residence, school, market, office, hospital, and transportation-related places.

PUBLIC PLACES

(1) RESIDENCE

집 [jip] : house

I live in a CHEAP house.

문 [mun] : door

I passed through the door to the MOON.

이웃 [i-ut] : neighbor

My neighbor is an INNUIT.

도시 [do-shi] : city

My friend lives in TOSHIba city.

방 [bang] : room

My room is messy as if the big BANG
exploded here.

잠 [jam] : sleep

After eating JAM, I go to sleep.

PLACES: RESIDENCE

bathroom 화장실 [hwa-jang-shil]

city 도시 [do-shi]

countryside 시골 [shi-gol]

door 문 [mun]

garbage 쓰레기 [sseu-re-gi]

hometown 고향 [go-hyang]

house 집 [jip]

kitchen 부엌 [bu-eog]

library 도서관 [do-seo-gwan]

life 생활 [saeng-hwal]

living room 거실 [geo-shil]

neighbor 이웃 [i-ut]

PLACES: RESIDENCE

Ⓝ park 공원 [gong-won]

Ⓝ playground 놀이터 [no-ri-teo]PR1.1

Ⓝ room 방 [bang]

Ⓝ sleep 잠 [jam]

Ⓝ town 동네 [dong-ne]

Ⓝ village 마을 [ma-eul]

Ⓝ window 창문 [chang-mun]

Ⓝ yard, garden 마당 [ma-dang]

Ⓥ hang (laundry) 널다 [neol-da]

Ⓥ spend time 지내다 [ji-nae-da]

Ⓐ noisy 시끄럽다 [shi-ggeu-reop-dda] PR1.3

Ⓐ quiet 조용하다 [jo-yong-ha-da]

(2) SCHOOL

학교 [hag-ggyo] PR1.3 : school
I will HUG YOU at school.

학생 [hag-ssaeng] PR1.3 : student
The student gave me a HUG and SANG a song.

선생님 [seon-saeng-nim] : teacher
My teacher's SON SANG NIMbly.

공부 [gong-bu] : study

I studied the GONG BOOk.

책 [chaeg] : book

I paid the book with a CHECK.

연구 [yeon-gu] : research

My research is on a YOUNG GOOse.

책상 [chaeg-ssang] PR1.3 : desk

I wanted to CHECK a SONG written on my desk.

의자 [ui-ja] : chair

I drank sWEET CHAi on the comfortable chair.

연필 [yeon-pil] : pencil

My pencil fell in love with a YOUNG PILL.

가방 [ga-bang] : bag

My bag exploded "KA-BANG!" and went up in smoke.

문제 [mun-je] : problem

MOON CHEss is no problem to play.

시험 [shi-heom] : exam

Being afraid of the exam, SHE ran HOME.

박사 [bag-ssa] PR1.3 : doctorate

I got my doctorate degree for developing a BAG SAfe.

이론 [i-ron] : theory

She has a theory about the IRON curtain.

알다 [al-da] : to know

She is a know-it-ALL.

가르치다 [ka-reu-chi-da] : to teach

For KARAoke, she teaches best.

(N) absence 결석 [gyeol-sseog] PR1.3

(N) assignment 숙제 [sug-jje] PR1.3

(N) attendance 출석 [chul-sseog] PR1.3

(N) bachelor 학사 [hag-ssa] PR1.3

(N) bag 가방 [ga-bang]

(N) bell 종 [jong]

(N) book 책 [chaeg]

(N) chair 의자 [ui-ja]

(N) class room 교실 [gyo-shil]

(N) collage, university 대학교 [dae-hag-ggyo] PR1.3

(N) content 내용 [nae-yong]

(N) desk 책상 [chaeg-ssang] PR1.3

	English	Korean	Pronunciation
N	doctorate	박사	[bag-ssa] PR1.3
N	education	교육	[gyo-yug]
N	elementary s.	초등학교	[cho-deung-hag-ggyo] PR1.3
N	exam	시험	[shi-heom]
N	explanation	설명	[seol-myeong]
N	friend	친구	[chin-gu]
N	grade (1st, 2nd)	학년	[hang-nyeon] PR3.1
N	grade (A, B, C..)	성적	[seong-jeog]
N	graduate school	대학원	[dae-ha-gwon] PR1.1
N	high s.	고등학교	[go-deung-hag-ggyo] PR1.3
N	kindergarten	유치원	[yu-chi-won]
N	knowledge	지식	[ji-shig]

PLACES: SCHOOL

major	전공	[jeon-gong]
master	석사	[seog-ssa] PR1.3
middle s.	중학교	[jung-hag-ggyo] PR1.3
pencil	연필	[yeon-pil]
problem	문제	[mun-je]
professor	교수님	[gyo-su-nim]
research	연구	[yeon-gu]
scholarship	장학금	[jang-hag-ggeum] PR1.3
school	학교	[hag-ggyo] PR1.3
student	학생	[hag-ssaeng] PR1.3
study	공부	[gong-bu]
teacher	선생님	[seon-saeng-nim]

PLACES: SCHOOL

(N)	theory	이론	[i-ron]
(N)	uproar, discipline	야단	[ya-dan]
(V)	go / attend	다니다	[da-ni-da]
(V)	tie, fasten	매다	[mae-da]
(V)	to know	알다	[al-da]
(V)	not to know	모르다	[mo-reu-da]
(V)	to learn	배우다	[bae-u-da]
(V)	to play	놀다	[nol-da]
(V)	to realize	깨닫다	[ggae-dat-dda] PR1.3
(V)	to teach	가르치다	[ga-reu-chi-da]
(Aj)	difficult	어렵다	[eo-ryeop-dda] PR1.3
(Aj)	easy	쉽다	[shwip-dda] PR1.3

EXERCISE

선생님 **1**   **a** to know

교수님 **2**   **b** university

공부 **3**   **c** book

책 **4**   **d** to teach

문제 **5**   **e** professor

대학교 **6**   **f** to learn

연구 **7**   **g** teacher

가르치다 **8**   **h** problem

배우다 **9**   **i** research

알다 **10**   **j** study

1-g, 2-e, 3-j, 4-c, 5-h, 6-b, 7-i, 8-d, 9-f, 10-a

집 is _____ in English.

도시 is _____ in English.

친구 is _____ in English.

A room is _____ in Korean.

A window is _____ in Korean.

A school is _____ in Korean.

to attend school : _____ 에 _____ .

The test is difficult. : _____이 _____ .

an easy explanation : 쉬운 _____

house, city, friend, 방, 창문, 학교, 학교, 다니다, 시험, 어렵
다, 설명

(3) MARKET

생산 [saeng-san] : production
To increase egg production, she SANG a SONg to the chickens.

짐 [jim] : load
JIM carried a heavy load.

돈 [don] : money
I have a TON of money.

시장 [shi-jang] : market
SHE JUMped into the market for shopping.

얼마 [eol-ma] : how much
How much the OIL MA'am?

물건 [mul-geon] : object
The object made of WOOL is GONE.

주인 [ju-in] : owner
The owner said the deal was a SHOE-IN.

손님 [son-nim] : customer
My SON is a NIMble customer.

PLACES: MARKET

(N) business 사업 [sa-eop]

(N) CEO 사장님 [sa-jang-nim]

(N) commerce, trade 장사 [jang-sa]

(N) customer/client 고객 [go-gaeg]

(N) deal 거래 [geo-rae]

(N) development 발전 [bal-jjeon] PR1.3

(N) economy 경제 [gyeong-je]

(N) factory 공장 [gong-jang]

(N) how much 얼마 [eol-ma]

(N) labor 노동 [no-dong]

(N) load, burden 짐 [jim]

(N) market 시장 [shi-jang]

merchant	상인	[sang-in]
money	돈	[don]
object	물건	[mul-geon]
owner	주인	[ju-in]
payment	결제	[kyeol-jje] PR1.3
price	가격	[ga-gyeog]
production	생산	[saeng-san]
property, wealth	재산	[jae-san]
purchase	구매	[gu-mae]
sales, selling	판매	[pan-mae]
store	매장	[mae-jang]
visitor	손님	[son-nim]

PLACES: MARKET

(v) put out, release   내놓다   [nae-no-ta]^{PR4.1}

(v) to buy   사다   [sa-da]

(v) to collect   모으다   [mo-eu-da]

(v) to lose   잃다   [il-ta]^{PR4.1}

(v) to pay   내다   [nae-da]

(v) to put, place   두다   [du-da]

(v) to seek   구하다   [gu-ha-da]

(v) to sell   팔다   [pal-da]

(v) to suffer   당하다   [dang-ha-da]

(Aj) hard, strenuous   힘들다   [him-deul-da]

(4) OFFICE

사무실 [sa-mu-shil] : office
SAM, YOU CHILLed the red wine at the office?

경찰 [gyeong-chal] : police
The police brings a GUN and SHELL to fight the crime.

사건 [sa-ggeon]^{Exception of PR1.3} : incident
I SAW a GUN in the incident.

고용 [go-yong] : employment
GO, YOUNG man, for your dreams in employment!

바쁘다 [ba-bbeu-da] : busy
They were busy to build the tower of BABEL.

일 [il] : work

I work with an EEL.

자 [ja] : ruler

Can you measure
the size of your JAW
with a ruler?

accident	사고	[sa-go]	
boss, employer	상사	[sang-sa]	
company	회사	[hwe-sa]	
co-worker	동료	[dong-nyo] PR3.4	
employee	직원	[ji-gwon]PR1.1	
employment	고용	[go-yong]	
fact	사실	[sa-shil]	
general	일반	[il-ban]	
incident, affair	사건	[sa-ggeon]PR1.3	
job	직업	[ji-geop]PR1.1	
meeting	회의	[hwe-ui]	
office	사무실	[sa-mu-shil]	

PLACES: OFFICE

(N) part 일부 [il-bu]

(N) police 경찰 [gyeong-chal]

(N) politics 정치 [jeong-chi]

(N) professional 전문가 [jeon-mun-ga]

(N) purpose 목적 [mog-jjeog]PR1.3

(N) responsibility 책임 [chae-gim]PR1.1

(N) ruler 자 [ja]

(N) survey, investigation 조사 [jo-sa]

(N) task, duty 업무 [eom-mu]PR3.3

(N) telephone 전화 [jeon-hwa]

(N) work 일 [il]

(V) to make someone do, to order 시키다 [shi-ki-da]

V	to take advantage of, use	이용하다	[i-yong-ha-da]
V	to accomplish	이루다	[i-ru-da]
V	to give	주다	[ju-da]
V	to give (formal)	드리다	[deu-ri-da]
V	to hang	걸다	[geol-da]
V	to happen	생기다	[saeng-gi-da]
V	to knock	두드리다	[du-deu-ri-da]
V	to take	받다	[bat-dda] PR1.3
V	to use	사용하다	[sa-yong-ha-da]
Aj	busy	바쁘다	[ba-bbeu-da]
Aj	urgent	급하다	[geu-pa-da]PR4.2

155

EXERCISE

얼마	1	a	to use
경제	2	b	production
물건	3	c	to buy
주인	4	d	to accomplish
생산	5	e	to call
사다	6	f	to sell
팔다	7	g	how much
사용하다	8	h	economy
이루다	9	i	object
걸다	10	j	owner

1-g, 2-h, 3-i, 4-j, 5-b, 6-c, 7-f, 8-c, 9-d, 10-e

시장 is _____ in English.

사무실 is _____ in English.

회의 is _____ in English.

A customer is _____ in Korean.

A load is _____ in Korean.

A telephone is _____ in Korean.

The owner gives the work. :

_____이 _____ 을 _____ .

The customer sells the object. :

_____이 _____ 을 _____ .

to take money : _____ 을 _____

market, office, meeting, 손님, 일, 전화기, 주인, 일, 주다, 손님, 물건, 팔다, 돈, 받다

(5) HOSPITAL

병원 [byeong-won] : hospital
BJORN WON another tennis match, but he ended up in the hospital.

건강 [geon-gang] : health
The CON GANG tried to cheat people by exploiting their health issues.

독 [dog] : poison
The DOG detects the poison.

소독 [so-dog] : disinfection

They used a SOwn DOG for disinfection.

약 [yag] : medicine

YUCK! This medicine tastes bad.

주사 [ju-sa] : injection

They made an injection with orange JUICE.

칼 [kal] : knife

I cut my finger because I recieved a CALL while using a knife.

아프다 [a-peu-da] : painful

The APE had a painful wound.

PLACES: HOSPITAL

bacteria	세균	[se-gyun]
condition	상태	[sang-tae]
counseling	상담	[sang-dam]
discover	발견	[bal-gyeon]
disinfection	소독	[so-dog]
doctor	의사	[ui-sa]
health	건강	[geon-gang]
hospital	병원	[byeong-won]
illness	병	[byeong]
injection	주사	[ju-sa]
knife	칼	[kal]
life	생명	[saeng-myeong]

medicine	약	[yag]
need, necessity	필요	[pi-ryo] PR1.1
nurse	간호사	[gan-ho-sa]
opinion	의견	[ui-gyeon]
patient	환자	[hwan-ja]
poison	독	[dog]
preparation	준비	[jun-bi]
radiation	방사선	[bang-sa-seon]
science	과학	[gwa-hag]
situation	상황	[sang-hwang]
surgery	수술	[su-sul]
technology	기술	[gi-sul]

N treatment 치료 [chi-ryo]

V to care for 위하다 [wi-ha-da]

V to finish 마치다 [ma-chi-da]

V to look carefully 살피다 [sal-pi-da]

V to suppress 참다 [cham-dda] PR1.3

V to throw away 버리다 [beo-ri-da]

V to wipe 닦다 [dag-dda] PR1.3

Aj durable 튼튼하다 [teun-teun-ha-da]

Aj painful 아프다 [a-peu-da]

Aj possible 가능하다 [ga-neung-hada]

Aj strong 강하다 [gang-ha-da]

(6) TRANSPORTATION -RELATED PLACES

CHA CHA ♪

차 [cha] : car

The car is dancing CHA-cha.

자리 [ja-ri] : room, space

There is some space for CHERRIes in the bowl.

길 [gil] : way, street

When the fish walked on the market street, its GILLs breathed with excitement.

거리 [geo-ri] : avenue

Fifth avenue has many CURRY restaurants.

벽 [byeog] : wall

I have a photo poster of BJÖRK on my wall.

가다 [ga-da] : to go

I couldn't make the CAmel go.

오다 [o-da] : to come

Everyone said "OH" when she came.

걷다 [geot-dda] PR1.3 : to walk

I put on my COAT when I go for a walk.

기다리다 [gi-da-ri-da] : to wait

I was waiting for the KEY DARIng to jump.

airplane	비행기	[bi-haeng-gi]
airport	공항	[gong-hang]
around	주위	[ju-wi]
automobile	자동차	[ja-dong-cha]
avenue	거리	[geo-ri]
bicycle	자전거	[ja-jeon-geo]
building	건물	[geon-mul]
bus	버스	[beo-seu]
car	차	[cha]
caution	주의	[ju-ui]
crack, gap	틈	[teum]
crosswalk	횡단보도	[hweng-dan-bo-do]

direction	방향	[bang-hyang]
floor	바닥	[ba-dag]
garage	주차장	[ju-cha-jang]
harbor	항구	[hang-gu]
motorcycle	오토바이	[o-to-ba-i]
parking	주차	[ju-cha]
pedestrian	보행자	[bo-haeng-ja]
road	도로	[do-ro]
room, space	자리	[ja-ri]
ship	배	[bae]
spacecraft	우주선	[u-ju-seon]
station	역	[yeog]

(N) (bus) station 정류장 [jeong-ryu-jang]

(N) structure 구조 [gu-jo]

(N) subway 지하철 [ji-ha-cheol]

(N) tour 관광 [gwan-gwang]

(N) traffic 교통 [gyo-tong]

(N) traffic light 신호등 [shin-ho-deung]

(N) train 기차 [gi-cha]

(N) travel 여행 [yeo-haeng]

(N) wall 벽 [byeog]

(N) way, street 길 [gil]

(V) to come 오다 [o-da]

(V) to fall, unload 내리다 [nae-ri-da]

PUBLIC PLACES: TRANSPORTATION

ⓥ to find   찾다   [chat-dda] PR1.3

ⓥ to float   뜨다   [ddeu-da]

ⓥ to follow   따르다   [dda-reu-da]

ⓥ to go   가다   [ga-da]

ⓥ to go through   통하다   [tong-ha-da]

ⓥ to head for   향하다   [hyang-ha-da]

ⓥ to ride   타다   [ta-da]

ⓥ to stand   서다   [seo-da]

ⓥ to stop   멈추다   [meom-chu-da]

ⓥ to turn, spin   돌다   [dol-da]

ⓥ to wait   기다리다   [gi-da-ri-da]

ⓥ to walk   걷다   [geot-dda] PR1.3

EXERCISE

아프다 1	a to go
가능하다 2	b to walk
가다 3	c to ride
오다 4	d to find
걷다 5	e painful
기다리다 6	f to come
서다 7	g to wait
타다 8	h to turn
찾다 9	i possible
돌다 10	j to stand

1-e, 2-i, 3-a, 4-f, 5-b, 6-g, 7-j, 8-c, 9-d, 10-h

병원 is _____ in English.

방향 is _____ in English.

차 is _____ in English.

Health is _____ in Korean.

A doctor is _____ in Korean.

A street is _____ in Korean.

*Some of the exercises might sound funny and sometimes doesn't make sense at all. But the funny pictures you imagine will help you to make strong associations.

The patient stops : _____ 가 _____ .

The knife enters : _____ 이 _____ .

The technology is strong : _____ 이 _____ .

hospital, direction, car, 건강, 의사, 길, 환자, 멈추다, 칼, 들어가다, 기술, 강하다

Koreans use two different number systems. Pure Korean numbers count from 1 to 100 and are commonly used to count objects, people, one's age, etc. Sino-Korean numbers are used for larger numbers, such as counting years, distances, money, etc. It can be challenging to learn both systems, but we developed a new approach to learn them with a smile.

NUMBERS

Before we start, we suggest that you revise the explanation for association-based learning in the introduction (Page 21). In this chapter, we will make use of a number-based association system that was developed by Henry Herdson in the 17th century, which John Sambrook extended by creating associations with similar-sounding syllables in the late 19th century.

1 one : bun

2

two : shoe

3

three : tree

4

four : door

5

five : hive

6

six : sticks

7

seven : heaven

8 eight : gate

nine : wine **9**

10 ten : hen

Did you get used to the number-based association system? Let's put it aside for a while, and meet these two characters: a cute girl and a Panda bear.

PURE KOREAN

SINO-KOREAN

As Koreans use two different number systems, pure Korean and Sino-Korean, it can be confusing to associate two different words with each word associated with a number. Thus, we are going to additionally associate a cute girl for pure Korean, and a Panda bear for Sino-Korean words. We thus have a triple association for (1) the number, (2) the little girl or the panda bear, and (3) the word for that number. For example, we will create an association between a bun representing the number 1, a little girl, and the word "Hana" which is the pure Korean word for the number 1. Although this may sound complicated at first, it has proved easy to memorize.

(1) PURE KOREAN NUMBERS

Below is a memory-aid story of a girl named Hana.

1 하나 [ha-na]
A little girl named HANA
baked a bun.

2

둘 [dul]

She also made a pair of shoes with a TOOL.

3

셋 [set]

Then she plants a SET of trees.

4 넷 [net]

She got tired, so she went to her house where the door is made of a NET.

181

5  다섯 [da-seot]

Next day, she met a bee in THE SUIT on its way back to the hive.

6

여섯 [yeo-seot]

She said "YOUR SUIT is made of sticks!"

Then the bee got angry and stung her.

7

일곱 [il-gop]

After she got ILL, GOD took her to heaven.

8 여덟 [yeo-deol]^{PR2.1}

At the gate, she sang
a YODEL song
and got better
again.

YODEL AY HEE HOO

9 아홉 [a-hop]

After she got better,
she says:
"I HOPE to swim in wine."

10

열 [yeol]

And then she was so happy that she tells her hens, "I love YOU ALL!"

PURE KOREAN NUMBERS

(Nu) one	하나	[ha-na]
(Nu) two	둘	[dul]
(Nu) three	셋	[set]
(Nu) four	넷	[net]
(Nu) five	다섯	[da-seot]
(Nu) six	여섯	[yeo-seot]
(Nu) seven	일곱	[il-gop]
(Nu) eight	여덟	[yeo-deol][PR2.1]
(Nu) nine	아홉	[a-hop]
(Nu) ten	열	[yeol]

Now, let's go over multiples of 10 up to 100. Since these are special only for pure Korean numbers, we do not need to form a triple association. For Sino-Korean numbers, the multiples of 10 are simply the number combined with the word for 10.

20

스물 [seu-mul]

When she turned twenty, she was still so SMALL.

30

서른 [seo-reun]

When she turned thirty, she was SO RUN down.

40
마흔 [ma-heun]

When she turned forty,
she called her husband
"MY HONey!"

50
쉰 [shin]

When she turned fifty,
she had problems with her SHIN.

60
예순 [ye-sun]

When she turned sixty,
she gave birth and said
"YES, SON"

70

일흔 [i-reun] ^{PR5 PR1.1}

When she turned seventy,
she retired and still said
"I RUN."

80

여든 [yeo-deun]

When she turned eighty,
she got a YACHT AND sailor.

90

아흔 [a-heun]

When she turned ninty,
she moved to AACHEN.

Nu	twenty	스물	[seu-mul]
Nu	thirty	서른	[seo-reun]
Nu	forty	마흔	[ma-heun]
Nu	fifty	쉰	[shin]
Nu	sixty	예순	[ye-sun]
Nu	seventy	일흔	[il-heun]
Nu	eighty	여든	[yeo-deun]
Nu	ninty	아흔	[a-heun]
V	to count	세다	[se-da]
V	to exceed	넘다	[neom-dda] PR1.3
V	to divide, share	나누다	[na-nu-da]

For numbers over 10, we can simply combine the word for the ten-decimal and single decimal number. For example, '열[yeol]:ten(10)' and '둘[dul]: two(2)' will make '열둘[yeol-dul]: twelve(12).'

열		둘		열둘
[yeol]	+	[dul]	➡	[yeol-dul]
ten (10)		two (2)		twelve (12)

열		넷		열넷
[yeol]	+	[net]	➡	[yeol-net]
ten (10)		four (4)		fourteen (14)

열		다섯		열다섯
[yeol]	+	[da-seot]	➡	[yeol-da-seot]
ten (10)		five (5)		fifteen (15)

In the same way, '스물[seu-mul]: twenty(20)' and '셋[set]: three(3)' will make '스물셋[seumul-set]: twenty-three(23).'

스물   셋   스물셋
[seu-mul] + [set] ➡ [seu-mul-set]
twenty (20)   three (3)   twenty-three (23)

서른   둘   서른둘
[seo-reun] + [dul] ➡ [seo-reun-dul]
thirty (30)   two (2)   thirty-two (32)

마흔   하나   마흔하나
[ma-heun] + [ha-na] ➡ [ma-heun-ha-na]
forty (40)   one (1)   forty-one (41)

(2) SINO-KOREAN NUMBERS

Sino-Korean numbers are the numbers originated from ancient Chinese. As most of the documents had been written in Chinese characters until Hangeul was created in 16th century, it may be a remaining habit to use Sino-Korean numbers in mathematics and official documents.

While pure Korean numbers are mostly written in Hangeul, Sino-Korean numbers are mostly written in Arabic numbers and are pronounced in the way indicated below.

0

영 [yeong]

We start growing from YOUNG age zero.

일 [il]

1

A panda ate a bun and became ILL.

2

이 [i]

He got a pair of E-shoes online and got better.

3

삼 [sam]

Then he fell asleep between SOME trees.

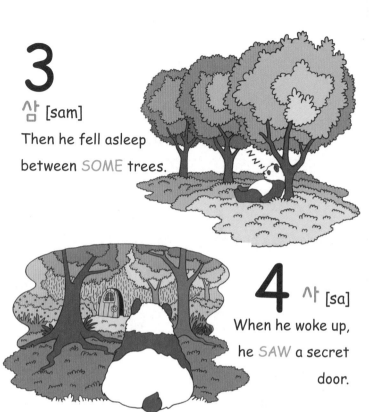

4

사 [sa]

When he woke up, he SAW a secret door.

5

오 [o]

Behind the door was a bee hive and he said "OH!"

OH!

6
육 [yug]

When hitting the hive with a stick, a bee flew into his mouth and he said "YUCK!"

7
칠 [chil]

Then he got afraid that he could not go to heaven and got a CHILL down his back.

8
팔 [pal]

At the gate beside him, he met his PAL.

9 구 [gu]

They shared some GOOey wine together.

10 쉽 [ship]

Then they went sailing on a SHIP full of hens.

SINO-KOREAN NUMBERS

(Nu) zero   공/영   [gong/yeong]

(Nu) one   일   [il]

(Nu) two   이   [i]

(Nu) three   삼   [sam]

(Nu) four   사   [sa]

(Nu) five   오   [o]

(Nu) six   육   [yug]

(Nu) seven   칠   [chil]

(Nu) eight   팔   [pal]

(Nu) nine   구   [gu]

(Nu) ten   십   [ship]

(N) number   숫자   [sut-ja]

It is easier to make the numbers bigger than 10 in Sino-Korean numbers compared to pure Korean numbers.

Do you remember that pure Korean numbers had each unique names for the multiples of 10? In Sino-Korean numbers, you can just put a suffix '-십[ship]', similar to '-ty' in English, for example 'six+ty' is 'sixty'. For example, combining '이[i]:two(2)' and '십[ship]:ten(10)' will make '이십[i-ship]:twenty(20).'

이		십		이십
[i]	+	[ship]	➡	[i-ship]
two (2)		ten (10)		twenty (20)

By using '십[ship]:ten(10)' as prefix, you can make numbers between the multiples of 10. For example, combining '십[ship]:ten(10)' and '이[i]:two(2)' will make '십이[shi-bi]:twelve(12).'

십
[ship]
ten (10)

+

이
[i]
two (2)

➡

십이
[shi-bi][PR1.1]
twelve (12)

(3) BIG NUMBERS

Now it is time for big numbers. As the numbers get bigger than thousand, the Korean number system becomes a little bit different from western numbers.

Western numbers have a special word for every exponent of base 1000: 1000^1 is thousand, 1000^2 is million, 1000^3 is billion, etc. The intermediate numbers are made with "ten" and "hundred", so we have for example ten thousand or hundred million.

On the other hand, Korean numbers have a special word for every exponent base 10000: 10000^1 is '만[man]', 10000^2 is '억[eog]', 10000^3 is '조[jo]', and so on. The intermediate numbers are made with '십[ship]' (=10), '백[baeg]' (=100), and '천[cheon]' (=1000), for example '백만[baeng-man]' is a million or '십억[shi-beog]' is a billion.

100

백 [baeg]

When she turned hundred,
she left on a long journey
with a BAG.

1,000

천 [cheon]

This city has thousand people called 'JOHN.'

10,000 만 [man]

This MAN has 10-thousand
friends on Facebook.

100,000,000 억 [eog]

There are 100million OAK trees in this forest.

1,000,000,000,000 조 [jo]

I have a trillion-dollar JOb.

We did not indicate numbers bigger than '조 [jo]' because they are barely used in ordinary circumstances.

100 hundred	백	[baeg]
1000 thousand	천	[cheon]
10000 ten thousand	만	[man]
100000 hundred thousand	십만	[shim-man]PR3.3
1000000 million	백만	[baeng-man]PR3.1
10000000 ten million	천만	[cheon-man]
100000000 hundred million	억	[eog]
1000000000 billion	십억	[shi-beog]PR1.1
10000000000 ten billion	백억	[bae-geog]PR1.1
100000000000 hundred billion	천억	[cheo-neog]PR1.1
1000000000000 trillion	조	[jo]

The rules of making variations to the big numbers is the same as that of Sino-Korean numbers. For example, combining '이[i]: two(2)' and '백[baeg]: hundred(100)' will make '이백 [i-baeg]: two-hundred(200).'

이		백		이백
[i]	+	[baeg]	➡	[i-baeg]
two		hundred		two-hundred
(2)		(100)		(200)

It goes the same with '천[cheon],' '만[man],' '억 [eog],' and '조[jo].'

For example, four hundred and thirty two thousand, seven hundred sixty five (432,765) is 사십삼만이천칠백육십오[sa-ship-sam-man-i-cheon -chil-baeg-yug-shi-bo][PR1.1].

Although it is more common to use Sino-Korean numbers for big numbers, sometimes you can also combine them with pure Korean numbers case by case.

For example, 'one-hundred twenty-two (122)' can either be '백스물둘 [baeg-seu-mul-dul]' as a pure Korean number, and '백이십이 [bae-gi-shi-bi][PR1.1]' as a Sino-Korean number.

EXERCISE

열여섯 1	a fifty-five (55)
스물하나 2	b sixteen (16)
마흔셋 3	c nine-hundred (900)
오십오 4	d twenty-one (21)
십일 5	e eleven (11)
이십이 6	f forty-three (43)
구백 7	g eighty-four (84)
여든넷 8	h thirty (30)
팔십구 9	i twenty-two (22)
삼십 10	j eighty-nine (89)

1-b, 2-d, 3-f, 4-a, 5-e, 6-i, 7-c, 8-g, 9-j, 10-h

삼백팔십 is _____ .

오억 is _____ .

칠십구 is _____ .

thirty-three (33) is _____ in Korean.

forty-eight (48) is _____ in Korean.

ninety-nine (99) is _____ in Korean.

count numbers : _____ 를 _____ .

exeed 10 : _____ 을(를) _____ .

three-hundred-eighty (380),
five-hundred-million (500,000,000), seventy-nine (79),
서른셋 (삼십삼), 마흔여덟 (사십팔), 아흔아홉 (구십구),
숫자, 세다, 열(십), 넘다

Knowing colors makes our world beautiful! In order to describe our beautiful world, we need to know the words of shapes. So let us learn colors and shapes in this chapter.

COLORS & SHAPES

(1) COLORS

Let's get started with the 7 basic 'Rainbow Colors.'

빨강 [bbal-gang] : red
The red BALL is GONE.

주황 [ju-hwang] : orange
I love drinking orange
JUICE in HONG Kong.

노랑 [no-rang] : yellow
There's a yellow sign
that says 'NO RUN'.

초록 [cho-rog] : green
JOE's ROCK is green.

파랑 [pa-rang] : blue
My PARENts love sailing under the blue sky.

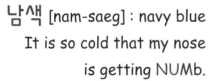

남색 [nam-saeg] : navy blue
It is so cold that my nose is getting NUMb.

보라 [bo-ra] : purple
The island of BORA-Bora is covered with purple flowers.

The following table explains the origin of the different color terms, some are pure Korean and some have their origin in Chinese. Knowing their origin can be important when composing words. The suffix '색[saeg]' means color and is often added for nouns.

	Pure Korean	Sino-Korean
black	Ⓝ검정(색) Ⓐⱼ검은	ⓃⒶⱼ흑색
blue	Ⓝ파랑(색) Ⓐⱼ파란	ⓃⒶⱼ청색
brown	ⓃⒶⱼ밤색	ⓃⒶⱼ갈색
green		ⓃⒶⱼ초록(색), 녹색
grey		ⓃⒶⱼ회색
navy blue	ⓃⒶⱼ곤색	ⓃⒶⱼ남색
orange		ⓃⒶⱼ주황(색)
pink		ⓃⒶⱼ분홍(색)
purple	ⓃⒶⱼ보라(색)	
red	Ⓝ빨강(색) Ⓐⱼ빨간	ⓃⒶⱼ적색, 홍색
white	Ⓝ하양(색) Ⓐⱼ하얀	ⓃⒶⱼ백색
yellow	Ⓝ노랑(색) Ⓐⱼ노란	ⓃⒶⱼ황색

The 5 basic colors — Red, Yellow, Blue, Black, and White — have different forms or ending-syllables depending on their grammatical usage. As nouns, they end with a consonant 'ㅇ[ng].' As adjectives, they end with 'ㄴ[n].' For example, 'red' as a noun is '빨강[bbal-gang],' and as an adjective, it is '빨간[bbal-gan].' One complication is in 'black', as its ending syllable '정[jeong]' transforms itself into '은[eun]' when used as an adjective.

The 🅐𝐟 marks on the right side of the following table indicates the Sino-Korean affixes representing each color.

214

COLORS

black	ⓝ검정 [geom-jeong] ⓐ검은 [geo-meun] PR1.1	ⓐf 흑 [heug]
blue	ⓝ파랑 [pa-rang] ⓐ파란 [pa-ran]	ⓐf 청 [cheong]
red	ⓝ빨강 [bbal-gang] ⓐ빨간 [bbal-gan]	ⓐf 적 [jeog], 홍 [hong], 주 [ju]
white	ⓝ하양 [ha-yang] ⓐ하얀 [ha-yan]	ⓐf 백 [baeg]
yellow	ⓝ노랑 [no-rang] ⓐ노란 [no-ran]	ⓐf 황 [hwang]

The warm-colors often include the three Sino-Korean affixes '적 [jeog]' or '홍 [hong]' or '주 [ju]' meaning 'red.'

On the contrary, the cool often include the three Sino-Korean affixes '청 [cheong]' meaning 'blue,' or '녹 [nog]' or '록 [rog]' meaning 'green.'

'색 [saeg]' can either serve as an affix or a word meaning 'color.' For some colors, it is optional to put it as a suffix, and for other colors, it is necessary as the table on Page 217 indicates.

COLORS

(N) color (casual)   색깔   [sae-ggal]

(N) color (formal)   색   [saeg]

(Aj) black   검다   [geom-dda] PR1.3

(Aj) blue, green   푸르다   [pu-reu-da]

(N)(Aj) blue-green   청록색   [cheong-nog-ssaeg]PR3.4

(N)(Aj) blue-grey   청회색   [cheong-hwe-saeg]

(Aj) bright   밝다   [bag-dda] PR1.3

(N)(Aj) brown   갈색   [gal-ssaeg] PR1.3

(Aj) dark   어둡다   [eo-dup-dda] PR1.3

(N)(Aj) deep-grey   진회색   [jin-hwe-saeg]

(N)(Aj) gold   금색   [geum-saeg]

COLORS

(N)(Aj) green
초록 [cho-rog]
녹색 [nog-ssaeg] PR1.3

(N)(Aj) grey
회색 [hwe-saeg]

(N)(Aj) light-grey
연회색 [yeon-hwe-saeg]

(Aj) muddy, blurry
흐리다 [heu-ri-da]

(N)(Aj) navy blue
곤색 [gon-saeg]
남색 [nam-saeg]

(N)(Aj) orange
주황 [ju-hwang]

(N)(Aj) pink
분홍 [bu-nong] PR6 PR1.1

(N)(Aj) plum
자주색 [ja-ju-saeg]

(N)(Aj) purple
보라 [bo-ra]

(Aj) red (blurry)
붉다 [bug-dda] PR1.3

COLORS

(N)(Aj) red-brown 적갈색 [jeog-gal-ssaeg] PR1.3

(N)(Aj) silver 은색 [eun-saeg]

(N)(Aj) sky blue 하늘색 [ha-neul-saeg]

(Aj) soft 연하다 [yeo-na-da]PR6 PR1.1

(N)(Aj) sprout green 연두 [yeon-du]

(Aj) thick 진하다 [ji-na-da]PR6 PR1.1

(Aj) vivid 선명하다 [seon-myeong-ha-da]

(Aj) white 희다 [hee-da]

(N)(Aj) yellow-brown 황갈색 [hwang-gal-ssaeg] PR1.3

황토색 [hwang-to-saeg]

(N)(Aj) yellow-green 황록색 [hwang-nog-ssaeg]PR3.4

(2) SHAPES

Three basic shapes — circle, triangle, and square have their pure Korean names.

동그라미	세모	네모
[dong-geu-ra-mi]	[se-mo]	[ne-mo]
circle	triangle	rectangle

'세모[se-mo]: triangle' and '네모[ne-mo]: square' are derived from the pure Korean numbers '셋[set]: 3' and '넷[net]: 4' as they indicate the number of edges of the shape. They are combined with '모[mo],' which is a pure Korean suffix meaning 'angle.'

Similar with pure Korean names, we can use the sino-Korean numbers for the number of angles. They are combined with a Sino-Korean suffix '각형 [ga-kyeong]PR4.2' meaning 'angular shape,' except '원 [won]' meaning 'circle' itself.

원(형)	삼각형	사각형
[won]	[sam-ga-kyeong]PR4.2	[sa-ga-kyeong]PR4.2
circle	triangle	rectangle

While the three basic shapes have both pure Korean and Sino-Korean names, the shape with more angles than 4 are only called by their Sino-Korean name. For example, a pentagon (5 edges) is '오각형 [o-ga-kyeong]PR4.2' made of '오 [o]: 5' and '각형[ga-kyeong]PR4.2'.

PURE KOREAN SHAPES

(N) circle   동그라미   [dong-geu-ra-mi]

(N) diamond   마름모   [ma-reum-mo]

(N) rectangle   네모   [ne-mo]

(N) triangle   세모   [se-mo]

SINO-KOREAN SHAPES

Ⓝ	circle	원(형)	[won]
Ⓝ	cone	원뿔	[won-bbul]
Ⓝ	cube	정육면체	[jeong-yug-myeon-che]
Ⓝ	cylinder	원기둥	[won-ki-dung]
Ⓝ	hexagon	육각형	[yug-ga-kyeong]PR4.2
Ⓝ	oval	타원	[ta-won]
Ⓝ	pentagon	오각형	[o-ga-kyeong]PR4.2
Ⓝ	rectangle	사각형	[sa-ga-kyeong]PR4.2
Ⓝ	sphere	구	[gu]
Ⓝ	square	정사각형	[jeong-sa-ga-kyeong]PR4.2
Ⓝ	triangle	삼각형	[sam-ga-kyeong]PR4.2

SHASPES

(N) bucket, cylinder	통	[tong]
(N) diagram	도표	[do-pyo]
(N) dot, point	점	[jeom]
(N) figure	도형	[do-hyeong]
(N) figure, appearance	모습	[mo-seup]
(N) form, shape	형태	[hyeong-tae]
(N) line	선	[seon]
(N) part, portion	부분	[bu-bun]
(N) pattern	무늬	[mu-nee]
(N) photo	사진	[sa-jin]
(N) picture	그림	[geu-rim]
(N) shape	모양	[mo-yang]

SHAPES

N side　　　　　　　면　　　[myeon]

Aj big, tall　　　　크다　　[keu-da]

Aj few, little　　　적다　　[jeog-dda] PR1.3

Aj high　　　　　　높다　　[nop-dda] PR1.3

Aj large, spacious　넓다　　[neol-dda] PR1.3

Aj long　　　　　　길다　　[gil-da]

Aj low　　　　　　낮다　　[nat-dda] PR1.3

Aj many, much　　많다　　[man-ta]

Aj short　　　　　짧다　　[jjap-dda] PR1.3

Aj small, narrow　좁다　　[jop-dda] PR1.3

Aj small, short　　작다　　[jag-dda] PR1.3

EXERCISE

검다 **1**		**a**	small
희다 **2**		**b**	long
붉다 **3**		**c**	line
선 **4**		**d**	bucket
통 **5**		**e**	red
모습 **6**		**f**	white
작다 **7**		**g**	black
짧다 **8**		**h**	high
길다 **9**		**i**	shape
높다 **10**		**j**	short

1-g, 2-f, 3-e, 4-c, 5-d, 6-i, 7-a, 8-j, 9-b, 10-h

색 is _____ in English.

점 is _____ in English.

모양 is _____ in English.

To be big is _____ in Korean.

To be many is _____ in Korean.

A circle is _____ in Korean.

The shape is long : _____ 이 _____ .

The bucket is small : _____이 _____ .

The square is blue : _____ 가(이) _____ .

color, point, shape, 크다, 많다, 동그라미(원), 모양, 길다, 통,
작다, 네모(사각형), 파랗다

Talking about weather is
always good for small talk.
In Korean culture,
many start their conversation
with weather such as:
오늘은 날씨가 어때요?
(How's the weather today?)
In this chapter, we are going to
learn about vocabulary related
to weather, geography, time and
space,
and days of the week.

TIME & NATURAL
SURROUNDINGS

(1) WEATHER

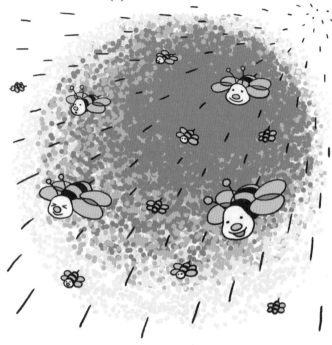

비 [bi] : rain

It rained like BEEs coming from the sky.

바람 [ba-ram] : wind

There was strong wind

when I left the BAR at 1 AM.

눈 [nun] : snow
It snowed at NOON.

하늘 [ha-neul] : sky
It is an HONOR to live up in the sky.

땅 [ddang] : ground
I stepped into DUNG on the ground.

따뜻하다 [dda-ddeu-ta-da]PR4.2 : warm
It is popular getting TATOO and TANned in a warm place.

덥다 [deop-dda] PR1.3 : hot (air)
It is hot on TOP of the tower.

무지개 [mu-ji-gae] : rainbow
Rainbow is the MUSIC-GAte.

(N) air	공기	[gong-gi]
(N) Autumn	가을	[ga-eul]
(N) cloud	구름	[gu-reum]
(N) dew	이슬	[i-seul]
(N) fog	안개	[an-gae]
(N) ground	땅	[ddang]
(N) light	빛	[bit]
(N) rain	비	[bi]
(N) rainbow	무지개	[mu-ji-gae]
(N) rainshower	소나기	[so-na-gi]
(N) season	계절	[gye-jeol]
(N) sky	하늘	[ha-neul]

WEATHER

(N) snow	눈	[nun]
(N) Spring	봄	[bom]
(N) Summer	여름	[yeo-reum]
(N) Sun	태양	[tae-yang]
(N) umbrella	우산	[u-san]
(N) weather	날씨	[nal-ssi]
(N) wind	바람	[ba-ram]
(N) Winter	겨울	[gyeo-ul]
(V) to blow	불다	[bul-da]
(V) to cover	덮다	[deop-dda]PR1.3
(V) to fall	떨어지다	[ddeo-reo-ji-da]PR1.1
(V) to pour	쏟아지다	[sso-da-ji-da] PR1.1
(V) to rise, float	떠오르다	[ddeo-o-reu-da]

ⓥ to stop, cease 그치다 [geu-chi-da]

Ⓐⱼ bright 밝다 [bag-dda]^{PR1.3 PR2.2}

Ⓐⱼ clear 맑다 [mag-dda]^{PR2.2}

Ⓐⱼ cloudy 흐리다 [heu-ri-da]

Ⓐⱼ cold (air) 춥다 [chup-dda]^{PR1.3}

Ⓐⱼ cold (object) 차갑다 [cha-gap-dda]^{PR1.3}

Ⓐⱼ cool 시원하다 [shi-won-ha-da]

Ⓐⱼ dark 어둡다 [eo-dup-dda]^{PR1.3}

Ⓐⱼ hot (air) 덥다 [deop-dda]^{PR1.3}

Ⓐⱼ hot (object) 뜨겁다 [ddeu-geop-dda]^{PR1.3}

Ⓐⱼ sunny 화창하다 [wha-chang-ha-da]

Ⓐⱼ warm 따뜻하다 [dda-ddeu-ta-da]^{PR4.2}

(2) GEOGRAPHY

산 [san] : mountain

I could see the SUNrise behind the mountain.

섬 [seom] : island

There are SOME islands nearby.

숲 [sup] : forest

Let's have some SOUP in the forest.

바다 [ba-da] : sea

The sea is full of BUTTER!

사막 [sa-mag] : desert

He SAW a MUG in the desert.

물 [mul] : water

A MULE is swimming in the water.

불 [bul] : fire

The BULL ran away from the fire.

GEOGRAPHY

Ⓝ area, countryside 지방 [ji-bang]

Ⓝ area, region 지역 [ji-yeog]

Ⓝ desert 사막 [sa-mag]

Ⓝ earth 지구 [ji-gu]

Ⓝ environment 환경 [hwan-gyeong]

Ⓝ fire 불 [bul]

Ⓝ forest 숲 [sup]

Ⓝ ice 얼음 [eo-reum] PR1.1

Ⓝ island 섬 [seom]

Ⓝ lake 호수 [ho-su]

Ⓝ mountain 산 [san]

Ⓝ nature 자연 [ja-yeon]

N		
river	강	[gang]
rock	바위	[ba-wi]
sand	모래	[mo-rae]
sea	바다	[ba-da]
soil	흙	[heug]^{PR2.2}
universe	우주	[u-ju]
water	물	[mul]
world	세계	[se-gye]
world	세상	[se-sang]
to appear	나타나다	[na-ta-na-da]
to block, stop	막다	[mag-dda] ^{PR1.3}
to catch (fire)	붙다	[but-dda] ^{PR1.3}

GEOGRAPHY

v to dig   파다   [pa-da]

v to disappear   사라지다 [sa-ra-ji-da]

v to gather   모이다   [mo-i-da]

v to leak, escape   새다   [sae-da]

v to step on   밟다   [bap-dda] PR1.3

v to turn off (light) 끄다   [ggeu-da]

Aj beautiful   아름답다 [a-reum-dap-dda] PR1.3

Aj clean   깨끗하다 [ggae-ggeu-ta-da] PR4.2

Aj deep   깊다   [gip-dda] PR1.3

Aj exist   있다   [it-dda] PR1.3

Aj not exist   없다   [eop-dda] PR1.3

Aj shallow   얕다   [yat-dda] PR1.3

EXERCISE

계절 1	a to dig
봄 2	b island
겨울 3	c forest
하늘 4	d season
빛 5	e clear
맑다 6	f to blow
불다 7	g light
파다 8	h winter
섬 9	i sky
숲 10	j spring

1-d, 2-j, 3-h, 4-i, 5-g, 6-e, 7-f, 8-a, 9-b, 10-c

바람 is _____ in English.

따뜻하다 is _____ in English.

자연 is _____ in English.

The sea is _____ in Korean.

Environment is _____ in Korean.

The world is _____ in Korean.

The water is deep. : _____ 이 _____ .

The rain pours. : _____ 가 _____ .

The cloud covers the mountain. :

_____ 이 _____ 을 _____ .

wind, warm, nature, 바다, 환경, 세계, 물, 깊다, 비,
쏟아지다, 구름, 산, 덮다

(3) TIME & SPACE

해 [hae] : sun

HEY, let's go out and see the sun coming up!

달 [dal] : moon

The moon shine was very DULL.

아침 [a-chim] : morning

Every morning she said: "AH JIM, please make me breakfast."

저녁 [jeo-nyeog] : evening

JOE KNOCKed on the door in the evening.

낮 [nat] : daytime

I tie a KNOT during daytime.

밤 [bam] : night

The BOMB exploded in the middle of the night.

(N)	a couple of days	며칠	[myeo-chil]
(N)	dawn	새벽	[sae-byeog]
(N)	day (reading calendar)	일	[il]
(N)	day	날	[nal]
(N)	days, years i.e. school days	시절	[shi-jeol]
(N)	daytime	낮	[nat]
(N)	east (side)	동(쪽)	[dong-jjog]
(N)	epoch, era	시대	[shi-dae]
(N)	evening, dinner	저녁	[jeo-nyeog]
(N)	future	미래	[mi-rae]
(N)	half	반	[ban]
(N)	lunch	점심	[jeom-shim]

(N) minute 분 [bun]

(N) modern times 현대 [hyeon-dae]

(N) moment 순간 [sun-gan]

(N) month (reading calendar) 월 [wol]

(N) moon, month 달 [dal]

(N) morning, breakfast 아침 [a-chim]

(N) night 밤 [bam]

(N) north (side) 북(쪽) [bug-jjog]

(N) one day 하루 [ha-ru]

(N) past 과거 [gwa-geo]

(N) present 현재 [hyeon-jae]

(N) second, beginning 초 [cho]

TIME & SPACE

(N) south (side)   남(쪽)   [nam-jjog]

(N) sun, year   해   [hae]

(N) time   시간   [shi-gan]

(N) time (reading clock) 시   [shi]

(N) today   오늘   [o-neul]

(N) tomorrow   내일   [nae-il]

(N) west (side)   서(쪽)   [seo-jjog]

(N) year (reading calendar) 년   [nyeon]

(N) yesterday   어제   [eo-je]

(V) to end, finish   끝나다   [ggeun-na-da] PR3.5

(V) to get up, happen   일어나다 [i-reo-na-da] PR1.1

(V) to start, begin   시작하다 [shi-ja-ka-da] PR4.2

TIME & SPACE

(V) to take (time)   걸리다 [geol-li-da]

(Aj) close, nearby   가깝다 [ga-ggap-dda] PR1.3

(Aj) early, soon   이르다 [i-reu-da]

(Aj) far   멀다 [mul-da]

(Aj) late   늦다 [neut-dda] PR1.3

(Av) at the same time   동시 [dong-shi]

(Av) for a moment   잠시 [jam-shi]

(Av) in those days   당시 [dang-shi]

(Av) now   지금 [ji-geum]

(Av) the old days   옛날 [yen-nal] PR3.5

(Av) then, now   이제 [i-je]

(C)(Pr) after   후 [hu]

TIME & SPACE

Pr back 뒤 [dwi]

C Pr before 전 [jeon]

Pr down 아래, 밑 [a-re], [mit]

Pr in front 앞 [ap]

Pr in the middle 가운데 [ga-un-de]

Pr in 안, 속 [an], [sog]

Pr left 왼쪽 [wen-jjog]

Pr out 밖 [bag]

Pr right 오른쪽 [o-reun-jjog]

Pr side 옆 [yeop]

Pr up 위 [wi]

(4) DAYS OF THE WEEK

월요일 [wo-ryo-il]^{PR1.1} : Monday
On Monday my apartment looked like a WAR zone.

화요일 [hwa-yo-il] : Tuesday
On Tuesday, my friends pulled a HOAx and threw a party in my apartment.

수요일 [su-yo-il] : Wednesday
After the noisy party, my neighbors SUEd me on Wednesday.

목요일 [mo-gyo-il]^{PR1.1} : Thursday
Then my neighbors MUGGed me on Thursday.

금요일 [geu-myo-il]^{PR1.1} : Friday
I stepped on GUM on Friday.

토요일 [to-yo-il] : Saturday

I dropped a hammer on my TOE on Saturday.

일요일 [i-ryo-il]^{PR1.1} : Sunday

I became ILL on Sunday.

What a great week!

DAYS OF THE WEEK

(N) Monday   월요일   [wo-ryo-il]PR1.1

(N) Tuesday   화요일   [hwa-yo-il]

(N) Wednesday   수요일   [su-yo-il]

(N) Thursday   목요일   [mo-gyo-il]PR1.1

(N) Friday   금요일   [geu-myo-il]PR1.1

(N) Saturday   토요일   [to-yo-il]

(N) Sunday   일요일   [i-ryo-il]PR1.1

(N) week day   요일   [yo-il]

(N) week (counting weeks) 주   [ju]

(N) weekend   주말   [ju-mal]

EXERCISE

해 1	a half
달 2	b yesterday
년 3	c year
월 4	d tomorrow
저녁 5	e minute
어제 6	f moon
내일 7	g evening
분 8	h then, now
반 9	i month
이제 10	j sun

1-j, 2-f, 3-c, 4-i, 5-g, 6-b, 7-d, 8-e, 9-a, 10-h

아침 is _____ in English.

어둠 is _____ in English.

지금 is _____ in English.

Lunch is _____ in Korean.

Today is _____ in Korean.

Time is _____ in Korean.

Yesterday, today and tomorrow :

_____ , _____ , 그리고 _____ .

Evening time : _____ _____

I eat lunch. : 나는 _____ 을 먹는다.

morning, darkness, now, 점심, 오늘, 시간, 어제, 오늘, 내일,
저녁, 시간, 점심

Living creatures on earth take up an important part of our lives. We need them for food, medicine, clothes, shelter, and as friends.

ANIMALS & PLANTS

(1) ANIMALS

Similar to western cultures, Koreans have good relationship with animals. Especially cats and dogs are popular pet animals.

Many animals have similar connotations as in western countries: fox is cunning, snails are slow, dogs are loyal, etc. Some animals, however, have different associations as indicated by the following stories.

In some Korean stories, rabbits are quite clever. There's a famous story called "별주부전", where the turtle tries to get the rabbit's liver to heal the King of the East sea. The rabbit tricks the turtle into believing that his liver is out to dry in his home and escapes the danger of death. In this case, the rabbit is even smarter than the turtle!

Another famous story is of the tiger and the dried persimmon (호랑이와 곶감), where a tiger ends up being afraid of dried persimmon! In that story, the tiger overhears a mother threatening her baby to be taken by a tiger if it doesn't stop crying then the baby cries even louder. But when the mother talks about dried persimmon, the baby stops crying and the tiger believes that dried persimmon must be even scarier!

Koreans have many proverbs with animals, many with frogs, dogs, and chickens. Here are some samples from the book "Looking for a Mr. Kim in Seoul" (서울에서 김서방 찾기), which is similar to the proverb "Looking for a needle in a haystack".

A frog in a well (우물 안 개구리) means a narrow-minded person, ignorant of the outside world.

After three years at a village schoolhouse, even a dog can recite a poem (서당개 삼 년에 풍월 읊는다) means practice makes perfect.

A country chicken (촌닭) is a person who cannot adjust to a new environment.

Even a monkey falls from the tree (원숭이도 나무에서 떨어진다) which means that even a master can make a mistake.

개 [gae] : dog
My dog is in a GAY mood.

말 [mal] : horse
I saw a horse at the MALL.

닭 [dag]PR2.2 : chicken
The chicken likes to TALK.

쥐 [jwi] : mouse, rat
GEEEz, there are so many rats in this house.

새 [sae] : bird
We SAY hello to the birds every morning.

뱀 [baem] : snake
This snake likes
BAMboo trees.

개미 [gae-mi] : ant
Ant soup tastes GAMEY.

거미 [geo-mi] : spider
The GUMMY spider is climbing up the wall.

벌레 [beol-le] : bug
Bugs are dancing
BALLET.

모기 [mo-gi] : mosquito
Mosquitoes stung me in MUGGY weather.

파리 [pa-ri] : fly
There are so many flies
in PARIs this year.

ANIMALS

(N) animal	동물	[dong-mul]
(N) animal, beast	짐승	[jim-seung]
(N) ant	개미	[gae-mi]
(N) baby (of an animal)	새끼	[sae-ggi]
(N) bird	새	[sae]
(N) bug	벌레	[beol-le]
(N) butterfly	나비	[na-bi]
(N) cat	고양이	[go-yang-i]
(N) chicken	닭	[dag]PR2.2
(N) cow	소	[so]
(N) dog	개	[gae]
(N) duck	오리	[o-ri]

ANIMALS

(N) egg   알(계란)   [al] (kye-ran)

(N) fish   물고기   [mul-go-gi]

(N) fish (for food)   생선   [saeng-seon]

(N) fly   파리   [pa-ri]

(N) food (for animals)   먹이   [meo-gi] PR1.1

(N) hawk   매   [mae]

(AV) horse   말   [mal]

(N) mosquito   모기   [mo-gi]

(N) mouse, rat   쥐   [jwi]

(N) nest   둥지   [dung-ji]

(N) pig   돼지   [dwae-ji]

(N) salmon   연어   [yeo-neo] PR1.1

ANIMALS

(N) shark	상어	[sang-eo]
(N) sheep	양	[yang]
(N) shrimp	새우	[sae-u]
(N) snake	뱀	[baem]
(N) spider	거미	[geo-mi]
(N) tail	꼬리	[ggo-ri]
(AV) tuna	참치	[cham-chi]
(N) whale	고래	[go-re]
(N) wing(s)	날개	[nal-gae]
(V) to bite	물다	[mul-da]
(V) to fly	날다	[nal-da]
(V) to give birth to	낳다	[na-ta] PR4.1

'알' together with a name of an animal simply refers to the egg of an animal. For example, a duck egg can be 오리알, which is a combination of 오리(duck) + 알 (egg). However, 달걀 is an exception. '달걀' is a word formed by a combination of Korean words. '닭' is a word for 'chicken,' '의' is a possessive particle which is 'of' in English, and '알' is 'egg.' Together, they make '달걀' meaning 'chicken egg.'

닭		알		달걀
[dag]PR2.2	+	[al]	➡	[dal-gyal]
chicken		egg		chicken egg

'계란' is another word for chicken egg, formed by a combination of Sino-Korean affixes. '계' is a prefix for 'chicken,' and '란' is a suffix for 'egg.' Neither of them can be used as independent words, but together, they form '계란.'

계		란		계란
[kye]	+	[ran]	➡	[kye-ran]
chicken		egg		chicken egg

'짐승돌' is another fun word to learn.

짐승	돌	짐승돌
[jim-seung] **+**	[dol] **➡**	[jim-seung-dol]
beast	idol	manly-idol

There have been many Korean boy bands with a large teenage fan-base since 90s. You can think of them as the Korean version of Backstreet Boys. The old trend was pretty childish, so Koreans called them '아이돌[aidol]' which can either mean the English word 'idol' or a compound of a Korean word '아이[ai]' (child) and the English word 'doll.'

However, the new trend nowadays is '짐승돌 [jim-seung-dol],' which is a compound of '짐승 [jim-seung]' (beast) and doll. They are manly boy bands with heaps of sex-appeal, for whom the main fan-base consists of grown-up woman fans called 이모팬, a compound of 이모(aunt) and 팬(fan). Similarly, we have 삼촌팬, where 삼촌 means "uncle" -- they are the older fans of girl bands!

As mentioned in Chapter 4, Koreans consider people as one big family, so everyone can be a brother, sister, uncle and aunt to them.

(2) PLANTS

Korea's four seasons provide distinct seasonal fruits. Among them is the Korean pear(배[bae]): brown, round, and as big as two fists. Pears are harvested around Chuseok '추석' (Korean Thanksgiving holiday around mid-September) and thus became one of Chuseok's specialties. 배 also means abdomen or belly, so when we think of 배(pear) we can also think of a big belly.

배 [bae] : pear
PEAr and 배 coincidently sound alike!

씨 [ssi] : seed
SEEd and 씨 also coincidently sound alike!

꽃 [ggot] : flower
A romantic GOAT loves flowers.

식물 [shing-mul]PR3.1 : plant
AstoniSHING MULberry plant

뿌리 [bbu-ri] : root
This BURRIto has roots inside.

가시 [ga-shi] : thorn
GOSH, the thorn hurt me.

논 [non] : rice paddy
NONE of them were in the rice paddy.

밀 [mil] : wheat
Wheat provides us
our daily MEAL.

PLANTS

apple   사과   [sa-gwa]

bean   콩   [kong]

branch   가지   [ga-ji]

carrot   당근   [dang-geun]

corn   옥수수   [og-su-su]

cucumber   오이   [o-i]

field   들   [deul]

flower   꽃   [ggot]

fruit   과일   [gwa-il]

garlic   마늘   [ma-neul]

grape   포도   [po-do]

grass   풀   [pul]

PLANTS

(N) lawn	잔디	[jan-di]
(N) leaf	잎	[ip]
(N) onion	양파	[yang-pa]
(N) pear	배	[bae]
(N) persimmon	감	[gam]
(N) plant	식물	[shing-mul]PR3.1
(N) potato	감자	[gam-ja]
(N) pumpkin	호박	[ho-bag]
(N) rice	쌀	[ssal]
(N) rice paddy	논	[non]
(N) root	뿌리	[bbu-ri]
(N) seed	씨	[ssi]

PLANTS

(N) spinach	시금치	[shi-geum-chi]
(N) sprout	싹	[ssag]
(N) stem	줄기	[jul-gi]
(N) strawberry	딸기	[ddal-gi]
(N) thorn	가시	[ga-shi]
(N) tree	나무	[na-mu]
(N) wheat	밀	[mil]
(N) vegetable	야채	[ya-chae]
(N) vegetable	채소	[chae-so]
(V) to bloom	피다	[pi-da]
(V) to grow	자라다	[ja-ra-da]
(V) to nip off	따다	[dda-da]

'밭 [bat]' is a word meaning 'field' which is commonly combined with the words for flowers, grass, or lawn.

꽃		밭		꽃밭
[ggot]	+	[bat]	➡	[ggot-bat]
flower		field		flower-field

풀		밭		풀밭
[pul]	+	[bat]	➡	[pul-bat]
grass		field		grass-field

잔디		밭		잔디밭
[jan-di]	+	[bat]	➡	[jan-di-bat]
lawn		field		large lawn

'싹 [ssag]' shares the same meaning with '새싹 [sae-ssag].' They are both commonly used as words for sprout.

새 + 싹 ➡ 새싹
[sae] + [ssag] ➡ [sae-ssag]
new + sprout ➡ sprout

It goes the same with '잎 [ip]: leaf' sharing the same meaning with '잎새 [ip-sae]' and '잎사귀 [ip-sa-gwi],' but '잎 [ip]: leaf' is more flexible in its plural usage, or when being combined with other words.

'양파 [yang-pa]' is formed by a combination of a prefix '양 [yang]: western' and a word '파 [pa]: green onion,' as the 'green onion' is considered to be the common one.

양		파		양파
[yang]	**+**	[pa]	➡	[yang-pa]
western		green onion		onion

Similarly with '상추 [sang-chu]' and '배추 [bae-chu]', which refer to 'Romaine lettuce' and 'Chinese cabbage'. Their corresponding western versions are expressed by placing '양 [yang]: western' in front of the Korean word.

양		상추		양상추
[yang]	**+**	[sang-chu]	➡	[yang-sang-chu]
western		Romaine lettuce		lettuce

양		배추		양배추
[yang]	**+**	[bae-chu]	➡	[yang-bae-chu]
western		Chinese cabbage		cabbage

EXERCISE

꼬리 1		a	horse
알 2		b	leaf
나무 3		c	root
뿌리 4		d	tree
가지 5		e	rice
잎 6		f	beast
씨 7		g	tail
짐승 8		h	branch
말 9		i	seed
쌀 10		j	egg

1-g, 2-j, 3-d, 4-c, 5-h, 6-b, 7-i, 8-f, 9-a, 10-e

새 is _____ in English.

개 is _____ in English.

나무 is _____ in English.

To grow is _____ in Korean.

To gather is _____ in Korean.

Bean is _____ in Korean.

A pig flies : _____ 가 _____ .

A flower falls. : _____ 이 _____ .

A sheep bites. : _____ 이 _____ .

bird, dog, tree, 자라다, 모이다, 콩, 돼지, 날다, 꽃, 떨어지다,
양, 물다

Good friendship and successful business in a foreign country start from understanding each other's culture. We can learn the culture from food, arts & literature, sports, relationships, religions & holidays.

10 CULTURE

(1) FOOD

In this section, we will introduce some of the traditional Korean foods.

Kimchi (김치) is a side dish made of fermented vegetables. There are hundreds of varieties of kimchi, and the ingredients differ depending on the type of kimchi being made.

It can be made from napa cabbage, radish, scallion, or cucumber as a main ingredient. The seasonings often include brine, scallions, spices, ginger, chopped radish, garlic, shrimp sauce, and fish sauce.

Bulgogi (불고기) literally means fire-meat. It is a main dish made of marinated meat. It can be made with beef, pork, chicken, duck, or any other kind of meat. The marinade sauce often includes soy-sauce, pepper, minced garlic, onion and ground fruits such as; apple, pear or kiwi.

People usually wrap a portion with a pickled radish cabbage slice and a leaf of lettuce or perilla, and then take a big bite.

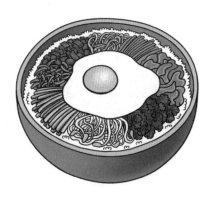

Bibimbab (비빔밥) is a casual dish made of rice and 4-5 different kinds of seasoned herbs and vegetables. It usually comes out with a fried egg or some Bulgogi on the top, often served with red pepper paste and sesame oil.

맛 [mat] : taste
The pizza is tasting like a floor MAT.

술 [sul] : alcohol
Alcohol brings out your SOUL.

꿀 [ggul] : honey

Honey with sunglasses is COOL.

김 [kim] : dried laver (seaweed)

Mr. KIM likes seaweed.

국 [gug] : soup

Let's COOK the soup.

식초 [shig-cho] : vinegar

The sour vinegar made the CHICK'S JAW drop.

떡 [ddeog] : ricecake

The DUCK likes ricecake.

기름 [ki-reum] : oil

Oil is the KEY to ROME.

후추 [hu-chu] : pepper

WHO CHEW the pepper?

(N) alcohol 술 [sul]

(N) beer 맥주 [maeg-ju]

(N) bibimbab 비빔밥 [bi-bim-bab]

(N) bulgogi 불고기 [bul-go-gi]

(N) cooking 요리 [yo-ri]

(N) culture 문화 [mun-hwa]

(N) deep-fry 튀김 [twi-gim]

(N) dried laver (seaweed) 김 [gim]

(N) floor table, award, prize, statue, mourning 상 [sang]

(N) food 음식 [eum-shig]

(N) herbs 나물 [na-mul]

FOOD

(N) honey	꿀	[ggul]
(N) kimchi	김치	[kim-chi]
(N) makgeolli	막걸리	[ma-ggeol-li]
(N) meal	식사	[shig-sa]
(N) meat	고기	[go-gi]
(N) oil	기름	[gi-reum]
(N) pepper	후추	[hu-chu]
(N) powder, flour	가루	[ga-ru]
(N) raw fish, sashimi	회	[hwe]
(N) red pepper paste	고추장	[go-chu-jang]
(N) rice cake	떡	[ddeog]
(N) rice, meal	밥	[bab]

FOOD

(N) salt   소금   [so-geum]

(N) sea mustard (sea-weed)   미역   [mi-yeog]

(N) soju   소주   [so-ju]

(N) soup   국   [gug]

(N) soybean paste   된장   [dwen-jang]

(N) steam   찜   [jjim]

(N) stir-fried rice cake   떡볶이   [ddeog-bbo-ggi] PR1.1

(N) stir-fry   볶음   [bo-ggeum] PR1.1

(N) sushi   초밥   [cho-bap]

(N) taste   맛   [mat]

(N) vinegar   식초   [shig-cho]

ⓥ to be drunk	취하다	[chwi-ha-da]
ⓥ to cool	식다	[shig-dda]$^{PR1.3}$
ⓥ to drink	마시다	[ma-shi-da]
ⓥ to eat	먹다	[meog-dda]$^{PR1.3}$
ⓥ to leave	남기다	[nam-gi-da]
ⓥ to mix	섞다	[seog-dda]$^{PR1.3}$
ⓥ to put in (a container)	담다	[dam-dda]$^{PR1.3}$
ⓥ to remain	남다	[nam-dda]$^{PR1.3}$
ⓥ to ripen	익다	[ig-dda]$^{PR1.3}$
ⓥ to shake, swing	흔들다	[heun-deul-da]
ⓥ to sprinkle	뿌리다	[bbu-ri-da]
ⓥ to starve	굶다	[gum-dda]$^{PR2.2\ PR1.3}$

'가루[ga-ru]: flour' has a large usage of making extended meanings, as well as its own meaning as an independent word.

쌀		가루		쌀가루
[ssal]	+	[ga-ru]	➡	[ssal-ga-ru]
rice		flour		rice flour

밀		가루		밀가루
[mil]	+	[ga-ru]	➡	[mil-ga-ru]
wheat		flour		wheat flour

(2) ARTS & LITERATURE

그림 [geu-rim] : drawing, painting
GRIMM brothers put some drawings in their book.

문학 [mun-hag] : literature
Reading literature is like receiving a MOON HUG.

신문 [shin-mun] : newspaper
He kicked the SHIN to the MOON.

소설 [so-seol] : novel
This novel was SO SOLd out.

옷 [ot] : clothes
He is wearing ODD clothes.

실 [shil] : thread
The SHIELD was made of thread.

ARTS & LITERATURE

(N) art 예술 [ye-sul]

(N) artwork 작품 [jag-pum]

(N) book 책 [chaeg]

(N) clothes 옷 [ot]

(N) concept 개념 [gae-nyeom]

(N) dance 춤 [chum]

(N) drawing, painting 그림 [geu-rim]

(N) experience 경험 [gyeong-heom]

(N) history 역사 [yeog-ssa] PR1.3

(N) idea 생각 [saeng-gag]

(N) inspiration, old man 영감 [yeong-gam]

(N) language 언어 [eo-neo] PR1.1

ARTS & LITERATURE

(N) letter, note	편지	[pyeon-ji]
(N) letter, type	글자	[geul-jja] PR1.3
(N) life	인생	[in-saeng]
(N) life, living	삶	[sam]PR2.2
(N) literature	문학	[mun-hag]
(N) meaning	의미	[ui-mi]
(N) music	음악	[eu-mag]PR1.1
(N) newspaper	신문	[shin-mun]
(N) novel, fiction	소설	[so-seol]
(N) paper	종이	[jong-i]
(N) plan	계획	[gye-hweg]
(N) poetry, poem	시	[shi]

(N) thread   실   [shil]

(N) work   작업   [ja-geop]^{PR1.1}

(N) writer   작가   [jag-gga]^{PR1.3}

(N) writing, text   글   [geul]

(V) to appear, show   나타내다   [na-ta-nea-da]

(V) to be empty   비다   [bi-da]

(V) to deliver   전하다   [jeon-ha-da]

(V) to draw   그리다   [geu-ri-da]

(V) to lay, place   놓다   [no-ta]^{PR4.1}

(V) to make   만들다   [man-deul-da]

(V) to put in   넣다   [neo-ta]^{PR4.1}

ARTS & LITERATURE

ⓥ to put on (clothes) 입다 [ip-dda]^PR1.3

ⓥ to put on (shoes) 신다 [shin-dda]^PR1.3

ⓥ to read 읽다 [ig-dda]^PR2.2 PR1.3

ⓥ to send 보내다 [bo-nae-da]

ⓥ to take off 벗다 [beot-dda]^PR1.3

ⓥ to take out 꺼내다 [ggeo-nae-da]

ⓥ to wear, slip on 걸치다 [geol-chi-da]

ⓥ to write, compose 쓰다 [sseu-da]

ⓥ to write, note 적다 [jeog-dda]^PR1.3

Ⓐ clear 분명하다 [bun-myeong-ha-da]

Ⓐ complex 복잡하다 [bog-ja-pa-da]^PR4.2

Ⓐ old, worn out 낡다 [nag-dda]^PR2.2 PR1.3

EXERCISE

국 1		a	alcohol
술 2		b	experience
맛 3		c	idea
문화 4		d	clothes
음악 5		e	soup
종이 6		f	to read
생각 7		g	paper
경험 8		h	culture
옷 9		i	taste
읽다 10		j	music

1-e, 2-a, 3-i, 4-h, 5-j, 6-g, 7-c, 8-b, 9-d, 10-f

만들다 is _____ in English.

신문 is _____ in English.

먹다 is _____ in English.

Culture is _____ in Korean.

A book is _____ in Korean.

A plan is _____ in Korean.

Draw a picture : _____ 을 _____ .

Write a letter : _____ 를 _____ .

Eat a meal : _____ 을 _____ .

to make, newspaper, to eat, 문화, 책, 계획, 그림, 그리다, 편지, 쓰다, 밥, 먹다

(3) SPORTS

모두 [mo-du] : all, everyone
This MODULE is for everyone.

적 [jeog] : enemy
The enemy likes to JOG.

끝 [ggeut] : end, finish
It feels GOOD to finish.

공 [gong] : ball
The GONG looks like a ball.

힘 [him] : strength

Spinach gives HIM strength.

원인 [wo-nin]^PR1.1 : reason

We WON IN the game for a good reason.

돌다 [dol-da] : spin

The ballerina DOLL is spinning.

던지다 [deon-ji-da] : throw

She threw out a TON of CHEESe.

SPORTS

(N) activity	활동	[hwal-ddong] PR1.3
(N) all, everyone	모두	[mo-du]
(N) ball	공	[gong]
(N) basketball	농구	[nong-gu]
(N) cause, reason	원인	[wo-nin] PR1.1
(N) center	중심	[jung-shim]
(N) competition	대회	[dae-hwe]
(N) effort	노력	[no-ryeog]
(N) end, finish	끝	[ggeut]
(N) enemy	적	[jeog]
(N) exercise, workout	운동	[un-dong]
(N) form	형식	[hyeong-shig]

SPORTS

(N) fun, interest   재미   [jae-mi]

(N) function, skill   기능   [gi-neung]

(N) gymnastics   체조   [che-jo]

(N) hiking, climbing   등산   [deung-san]

(N) method, way   방법   [bang-beop]

(N) practice   연습   [yeon-seup]

(N) record   기록   [gi-rog]

(N) result   결과   [gyeol-gwa]

(N) soccer   축구   [chug-gu]

(N) start, begin   시작   [shi-jag]

(N) step, walk   걸음   [geo-reum][PR1.1]

(N) strength   힘   [him]

SPORTS

(N) string, line 줄 [jul]

(N) swimming 수영 [su-yeong]

(N) the last 마지막 [ma-ji-mag]

(N) unit, measure 단위 [dan-wi]

(N) war 전쟁 [jeon-jaeng]

(N) whole 전체 [jeon-che]

(V) to avoid 피하다 [pi-ha-da]

(V) to carry 들다 [deul-da]

(V) to continue 계속하다 [gye-so-ka-da] PR4.1

(V) to endure 견디다 [gyeon-di-da]

(V) to get hit, to be right 맞다 [mat-dda] PR1.3

(V) to grow, increase 늘다 [neul-da]

(V) to jump	뛰다	[ddwi-da]
(V) to pull	끌다	[ggeul-da]
(V) to push	밀다	[mil-da]
(V) to run	달리다	[dal-li-da]
(V) to throw	던지다	[deon-ji-da]
(Aj) needed	필요하다	[pi-ryo-ha-da]
(Aj) quick	빠르다	[bba-reu-da]
(Aj) severe	심하다	[shim-ha-da]
(Aj) slow	느리다	[neu-ri-da]
(Av) instead of	대신	[dae-shin]
(Av) next	다음	[da-eum]

(4) RELATIONSHIPS

사이 [sa-i] : space, relationship
Drinking apple CIder is good for making relationships.

차이 [cha-i] : difference
Can you tell the difference between CHAI tea and black tea?

사진 [sa-jin] : photo
He SAW JEANs in the photo.

기회 [ki-hwe] : opportunity
It is an opportunity to eat KIWI.

대답 [dae-dap] : answer
Answer to my DAD, UP there!

혼자 [hon-ja] : alone
I like to drive alone in my HONDA car.

약속 [yag-ssog] : promise
Grandpa promised me to buy YAK SOCKs.

비밀 [bi-mil] : secret
It is a secret that I like BEE MEAL.

중요하다 [jung-yo-ha-da] : important
It is important to survive JUNIOR high.

이해하다 [i-hae-ha-da] : understand
EE-YAY! I understand!

RELATIONSHIPS

(N) alone   혼자   [hon-ja]

(N) answer, reply   대답   [dae-dap]

(N) appointment, promise   약속   [yag-ssog] PR1.3

(N) atmosphere, mood   분위기 [bun-wi-gi]

(N) attitude, manner   태도   [tae-do]

(N) change   변화   [byeon-hwa]

(N) condition, terms   조건   [jo-ggeon]

(N) difference   차이   [cha-i]

(N) fight, argument   싸움   [ssa-um]

(N) greeting   인사   [in-sa]

(N) influence   영향   [yeong-hyang]

(N) interest, attention   관심   [gwan-shim]

RELATIONSHIPS

ⓝ likewise   마찬가지 [ma-chan-ga-ji]

ⓝ news   소식   [so-shig]

ⓝ opportunity, chance 기회   [gi-hwe]

ⓝ personality   성격   [seong-gyeog]

ⓝ photo   사진   [sa-jin]

ⓝ process   과정   [gwa-jeong]

ⓝ relationship   관계   [gwan-gye]

ⓝ request, favor   부탁   [bu-tag]

ⓝ secret   비밀   [bi-mil]

ⓝ space, relationship 사이   [sa-i]

ⓝ story, conversation 이야기 [i-ya-gi]

ⓝ target, subject   대상   [dae-sang]

RELATIONSHIPS

(v) to ask 묻다 [mut-dda] PR1.3

(v) to fight 싸우다 [ssa-u-da]

(v) to hug 안다 [an-dda] PR1.3

(v) to meet 만나다 [man-na-da]

(v) to say 말하다 [mal-ha-da]

(v) to treat 대하다 [dae-ha-da]

(v) to understand 이해하다 [i-hae-ha-da]

(Aj) envious 부럽다 [bu-reop-dda] PR1.3

(Aj) glad (to meet sb) 반갑다 [ban-gap-dda] PR1.3

(Aj) important 중요하다 [jung-yo-ha-da]

(Aj) sorry 미안하다 [mi-an-ha-da]

(Aj) thankful 고맙다 [go-map-dda] PR1.3

(5) RELIGIONS & HOLIDAYS

자유 [ja-yu] : freedom
I have my freedom to give my JAR to YOU.

죽음 [ju-geum]PR1.1 : death
He CHEWED GUM until his death.

죄 [jwe] : crime, sin
If you commit a crime, you go to JAIl.

이유 [i-yu] : reason
There is a reason why EU exists.

설명 [seol-myeong] : explain
He explained how to catch a SALMON.

잊다 [it-dda]^{PR1.3} : forget
Don't forget IT.

다르다 [da-reu-da] : different
DARE to be different.

믿다 [mit-dda]^{PR1.3} : believe
I cannot believe it is not MEAT!

변하다 [byeo-na-da]^{PR5 PR1.1} : change
It is time to change our PIANo to a bigger one.

(N) buddhist temple 절 [jeol]

(N) ceremony 의식 [ui-shig]

(N) church (catholic) 성당 [seong-dang]

(N) church (protestant) 교회 [gyo-hwe]

(N) crime, sin 죄 [jwe]

(N) death 죽음 [ju-geum]PR1.1

(N) fortune, fate 운 [un]

(N) freedom 자유 [ja-yu]

(N) god 신 [shin]

(N) group 집단 [jip-ddan]PR1.3

(N) ideology, idea 사상 [sa-sang]

(N) luck, fortune 복 [bog]

(N) New Year's day   설   [seol]

(N) opinion, argument   주장   [ju-jang]

(N) organization   기관   [gi-gwan]

(N) paradise   낙원   [na-gwon]PR1.1

(N) party   잔치   [jan-chi]

(N) philosophy   철학   [cheo-rak]PR5 PR1.1

(N) reality   현실   [hyeon-shil]

(N) reason   이유   [i-yu]

(N) reason   까닭   [gga-dag]PR2.2

(N) religion   종교   [jong-gyo]

(N) society   사회   [sa-hwe]

(N)(A) strange, ideal, more than   이상   [i-sang]

(N) temple 신전 [shin-jeon]

(N) Thanksgiving day 추석 [chu-seog]

(N) truth, reality 실제 [shil-jje] PR1.3

(N) unification 통일 [tong-il]

(N) virtue 덕 [deog]

(V) to believe 믿다 [mit-dda]PR1.3

(V) to change 변하다 [byeon-ha-da]

(V) to change, switch 바꾸다 [ba-ggu-da]

(V) to connect 잇다 [it-dda]PR1.3

(V) to forget 잊다 [it-dda]PR1.3

(Aj) different 다르다 [da-reu-da]

(Aj) right 옳다 [ol-ta]PR4.1

EXERCISE

달리다 **1**		**a**	to continue
들다 **2**		**b**	photo
계속하다 **3**		**c**	alone
이야기 **4**		**d**	to carry
혼자 **5**		**e**	to run
사진 **6**		**f**	freedom
대답 **7**		**g**	to believe
만나다 **8**		**h**	to meet
자유 **9**		**i**	answer
믿다 **10**		**j**	story

1-e, 2-d, 3-a, 4-j, 5-c, 6-b, 7-i, 8-h, 9-f, 10-g

원인 is _____ in English.

힘 is _____ in English.

빠르다 is _____ in English.

Interest is _____ in Korean.

An opportunity is _____ in Korean.

A secret is _____ in Korean.

Throw a ball. : _____ 을 _____ .

Forget the appointment. :

_____ 을 _____ .

Understand the enemy. :

_____ 을 _____ .

cause, strength, quick, 관심, 기회, 비밀, 공, 던지다,
약속, 잊다, 적, 이해하다

Knowing conjunctions
and interjections
helps to understand
the context of dialogs.
Korean people, with their
language full of emotion,
use a lot of conjunctions
and interjections.

CONJUNCTIONS
& INTERJECTIONS

(1) CONJUNCTIONS

그러나 [geu-reo-na] : but
I like CORONA, but there is only Budweiser.

그래서 [geu-rae-seo] : so
The boy ate too many cookies so that his hands became GREASY.

만약 [ma-nyag]PR1.1 : if
If you are MANIAC, then read this book in one day.

함께 [ham-gge] : with, together
We are eating HAM with CAKE together.

아마 [a-ma] : perhaps
Perhaps we should say AMEn.

CONJUNCTIONS

also	또한	[ddo-han]
and	그리고	[geu-ri-go]
because	왜냐하면	[wae-nya-ha-myeon]
but	그러나	[geu-reo-na]
for	위해	[wi-hae]
hence	그러니까	[geu-reo-ni-gga]
how	어떻게	[eo-ddeo-ke]PR4.1
if	만약	[ma-nyag]PR1.1
moreover	게다가	[ge-da-ga]
or	또는	[ddo-neun]
perhaps	아마	[a-ma]
so, hence	그래서	[geu-rae-seo]

CONJUNCTIONS

therefore | 그러므로 | [geu-reo-meu-ro]

what | 무엇 | [mu-eot]

when | 언제 | [eon-je]

where | 어디에 | [eo-di-e]

which | 어떤 | [eo-ddeon]

who | 누구 | [nu-gu]

why | 왜 | [wae]

with, together | 함께 | [ham-gge]

yet | 아직 | [a-jig]

(2) INTERJECTIONS

INTERJECTIONS

In gosh	맙소사	[map-so-sa]
In no	아니오	[a-ni-o]
In oops	아이고	[a-i-go]
In ouch	아야	[a-ya]
In phew	휴	[hyu]
In please	제발	[je-bal]
In sure	물론	[mul-lon]
In uggh	윽	[eug]
In wow	우와	[u-wa]
In yes	예	[ye]
In yikes	으악	[eu-ag]

EXERCISE

그리고	1	a	yet
만약	2	b	and
아직	3	c	with
예	4	d	no
왜냐하면	5	e	if
누구	6	f	yes
함께	7	g	perhaps
아니오	8	h	because
아마	9	i	why
왜	10	j	who

1-b, 2-e, 3-a, 4-f, 5-h, 6-j, 7-c, 8-d, 9-g, 10-i

언제 is _____ in English.

물론 is _____ in English.

제발 is _____ in English.

Together is _____ in Korean.

Wow is _____ in Korean.

Ouch is _____ in Korean.

when, sure, please, 함께, 우와, 아야

Although it might seem
quite advanced,
it is very useful
to learn the affixes
since they form
components of a
large part of Korean
vocabulary.

AFFIXES

In this chapter, we will introduce the most important and basic affixes — both Sino-Korean and pure Korean affixes that are widely used to compose Korean words. An affix can be combined with a noun or a verb to make a new word. In this book, we'll mostly introduce affix groups that are used with nouns.

It may seem that learning different affixes may give more headaches to a Korean learner. However, once you grasp the basic concept, it will help you learn two or more words at the same time.

For example, if you know that a noun N + 가 is someone who is a specialist, you can guess what '교육가' is. With '교육' meaning education, '교육가' becomes an educator.

교육   가   교육가
[gyo-yug] +   [ga]   ➡   [gyo-yug-ga]
education   specialist   educator

(1) PERSONAL AFFIXES

First of all, we are going to introduce suffixes that indicate professions and characteristics of people. Intuitively, suffixes in this category can be English equivalents of –er, -or, -ist.

Suffixes -가, -사, -자, -수, -원 and -인 with a noun make another noun that represents someone who is proficient in something. In turn, most of the words developed in this way make words for jobs.

가 [ga] : expert, house

'가[ga]'(家) literally means a house. It indicates a high level of proficiency, referring to a large amount of time and artistic inspirations.

작 [jag] creation + 가 [ga] specialist ➡ 작가 [jag-gga]PR1.3 artist(writer)

작곡 [jag-ggog] composition + 가 [ga] specialist ➡ 작곡가 [jag-ggog-gga]PR1.3 composer

사 [sa] : scholar, job

'사 [sa]' (士 and 師)[6] literally means a scholar and a job. Jobs ending with 사 usually require a certain degree of education.

의   사   의사

[ui] **+** [sa] ➡️ [ui-sa]

cure   job   doctor

변호   사   변호사

[byeon-ho] **+** [sa] ➡️ [byeon-ho-sa]

advocacy   job   lawyer

---

6. Some Korean words use affixes that have the same sound and meaning but different characters, which most native Korean speakers do not recognize. For simplicity, we introduce these suffixes in the same category.

자 [ja] : person, thing

'자 [ja]' (者) means a person. It indicates a high level of proficiency, referring to a certain field that a person is working for.

과학 [gwa-hag] science

+

자 [ja] person

➡ 과학자 [gwa-hag-jja]PR1.3 scientist

기 [ki] record

+

자 [ja] person

➡ 기자 [ki-ja] journalist

수 [su] : hand, talent

'수 [su]' (手) literally means a hand and talent, referring a person who has a special talent.

가		수		가수
[ga]	+	[su]	➡	[ga-su]
sing		talent		singer

선		수		선수
[seon]	+	[su]	➡	[seon-su]
chosen		talent		athlete

교		수		교수
[kyo]	+	[su]	➡	[kyo-su]
teach		talent		professor

원 [won] : person, people

'원 [won]' (員) means a person who works usually for an institution or the government.

연구
[yeon-gu]
research

＋

원
[won]
officer

➡

연구원
[yeon-gu-won]
researcher

공무
[gong-mu]
public affairs

＋

원
[won]
officer

➡

공무원
[gong-mu-won]
public official

승무
[seung-mu]
on-board affairs

＋

원
[won]
officer

➡

승무원
[seung-mu-won]
crew member

인 [in] : human

'인 [in]' (人) literally means human. A nation + 인 refers to a person's nationality as we mentioned in Chapter 2.

외국		인		외국인
[we-gug]	**+**	[in]	➡	[we-gu-gin][PR1.1]
foreign		person		foreigner

'인' of −국+인 can be simply replaced by '사람' meaning a person in pure Korean. For example '한국인=한국사람'(Korean). Note that Nation+ 인 does not indicate gender of a person unlike some other languages.

However, a word indicating gender cannot be used with 인 or 사람. In other words, a female American should be 미국여자 not 미국여자사람 or 미국여자인.

꾼 [ggun] : expert

'꾼 [ggun]' is a pure Korean suffix. It refers to someone who is good at something or someone who is doing something habitually.

나무		꾼		나무꾼
[na-mu]	+	[ggun]	➡	[na-mu-ggun]
tree		skilled person		lumberjack

사기		꾼		사기꾼
[sa-gi]	+	[ggun]	➡	[sa-gi-ggun]
fraud		skilled person		fraudster

사냥		꾼		사냥꾼
[sa-nyang]	+	[ggun]	➡	[sa-nyang-ggun]
hunt		skilled person		hunter

꾸러기[ggu-reo-gi], 쟁이[jaeng-i], 보[bo]

'꾸러기 [ggu-reo-gi]', '쟁이 [jaeng-i]', and '보 [bo]' refer to someone who overdoes something in a cute way. They are usually used for little children. The difference is that 꾸러기 and 쟁이 comes with a noun whereas 보 uses a stem of a verb to make a new noun.

잠	+	꾸러기	➡	잠꾸러기
[jam]		[ggu-reo-gi]		[jam-ggu-reo-gi]
sleep		person		sleepyhead

욕심	+	쟁이	➡	욕심쟁이
[yog-shim]		[jaeng-i]		[yog-shim-jaeng-i]
greed		person		greedy child

울(다)	+	보	➡	울보
[ulda]		[bo]		[ul-bo]
cry		person		crybaby

(N) acquaintance   지인   [ji-in]

(N) alien   외계인   [we-gye-in]

(N) artist, writer   작가   [jag-gga][PR1.3]

(N) astronaut   우주인   [u-ju-in]

(N) athlete   선수   [seon-su]

(N) composer   작곡가   [jag-gog-gga][PR1.3]

(N) coward   겁쟁이   [geop-jaeng-i]

(N) crew member   승무원   [seung-mu-won]

(N) crybaby   울보   [ul-bo]

(N) doctor   의사   [ui-sa]

(N) driver   기사   [ki-sa]

(N) elderly   노인   [no-in]

HUMAN

ⓝ fool	바보	[ba-bo]
ⓝ foreigner	외국인	[we-gu-gin]^{PR1.1}
ⓝ fraudster	사기꾼	[sa-gi-ggun]
ⓝ grabber	욕심쟁이	[yog-shim-jaeng-i]
ⓝ host, owner	주인	[ju-in]
ⓝ hunter	사냥꾼	[sa-nyang-ggun]
ⓝ journalist	기자	[ki-ja]
ⓝ lawyer	변호사	[byeo-no-sa]^{PR5 PR1.1}
ⓝ local resident	내국인	[nae-gu-gin]^{PR1.1}
ⓝ lumberjack	나무꾼	[na-mu-ggun]
ⓝ merchant	상인	[sang-in]
ⓝ mischievous child	장난꾸러기	[jang-nan-ggu-reo-gi]

(N) others, stranger	타인	[ta-in]
(N) poet	시인	[shi-in]
(N) professor	교수	[kyo-su]
(N) public official	공무원	[gong-mu-won]
(N) researcher	연구원	[yeon-gu-won]
(N) scholar	학자	[hag-jja]PR1.3
(N) schoolteacher	교사	[kyo-sa]
(N) scientist	과학자	[gwa-hag-jja]PR1.3
(N) singer	가수	[ga-su]
(N) sleepyhead	잠꾸러기	[jam-ggu-reo-gi]
(N) the beauty	미인	[mi-in]
(N) the deceased	고인	[go-in]

(2) NUMERAL AFFIXES

Now, we will introduce some numeral affixes.

번 [beon] : suffix for number of times

With a suffix '번 [beon],' you can use the numbers to count 'how many times'. Some numbers will have small changes — getting rid of the last consonant or vowel — to be combined with '번 [beon]':

'하나[ha-na]:one' looses its last vowel 'ㅏ[a]' and becomes '한 [han].'

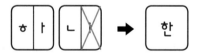

'한 [han]' meets the suffix '번 [beon]' and makes '한번 [han-beon]: one time'

'둘[dul]:two' looses its last consonant 'ㄹ[l]' and becomes '두[du].' Then it meets the suffix '번 [beon]' and makes '두번 [du-beon]: two times'

'셋[set]:three' and '넷[net]:four' loose their 'ㅅ [t]' and become '세[se]' and '네[ne]' to make '세 번 [se-beon]: three times' and '네번 [ne-beon]: four times.'

'스물[seu-mul]:twenty' looses its 'ㄹ[l]' and becomes '스무[seu-mu].'

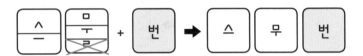

For the rest of the numbers, just add '번 [beon].' For example, '다섯[da-seot]:five' becomes '다섯번 [da-seot-beon]: five times,' '여섯 [yeo-seot]:six' becomes '여섯번 [yeo-seot-beon]: six times,' and so on.

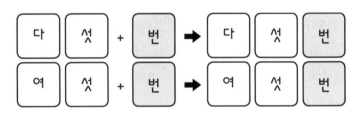

개 [gae] : suffix for things

The suffix '개 [gae]' will enable the numbers to count 'how many things'. It works the same as the suffix '번 [beon].'

한		개		한개
[han]	+	[gae]	➡	[han-gae]
one		thing		one thing

두		개		두개
[du]	+	[gae]	➡	[du-gae]
two		thing		two things

세		개		세개
[se]	+	[gae]	➡	[se-gae]
three		thing		three things

가지 [ga-ji] : suffix for kinds

잔 [jan] : suffix for cups of drink

명 [myeong] : suffix for people

분 [bun] : suffix for people(formal)

마리 [ma-ri] : suffix for animals

그루 [geu-ru] : suffix for trees

송이 [song-i] : suffix for flowers

곳 [got] : suffix for places

All these suffixes work the same way as the suffixes '번 [beon]' and '개 [gae].'

한		가지		한가지
[han]	+	[ga-ji]	➡	[han-ga-ji]
one		kind		one kind

두		잔		두잔
[du]	+	[jan]	➡	[du-jan]
two		cup		two cups of drink

세		명		세명
[se]	+	[myeong]	➡	[se-myeong]
three		person		three people

네		마리		네마리
[ne]	+	[ma-ri]	➡	[ne-ma-ri]
four		animal		four animals

다섯		송이		다섯송이
[da-seot]	+	[song-i]	➡	[da-seot-song-i]
five		flower		five flowers

째 [jjae] : ordinal suffix

By adding a suffix '째 [jjae],' you can make ordinal numbers.

Number 'one' is special, as '첫 [cheot]' replaces '하나[ha-na],' combined with '째 [jjae]' makes '첫째[cheot-jjae]' meaning 'first.'

첫		째		첫째
[cheot]	**+**	[jjae]	**➡**	[cheot-jjae]
first		ordinal		first (1st)

For the rest, just adding a suffix '째 [jjae]' on each numbers will work.

둘		째		둘째
[dul]	**+**	[jjae]	**➡**	[dul-jjae]
two		ordinal		second (2nd)

번째 [beon-jjae] : ordinal suffix

Combining the two suffixes, '번 [beon]' and
'째 [jjae]' also works as ordinal numbers. The
word-combining rule is the same as '번 [beon]'.

첫　　　　번째　　　　첫번째
[cheot] + [beon-jjae] ➡ [cheot-beon-jjae]
first　　　ordinal　　　first time

둘　　　　번째　　　　두번째
[dul] + [beon-jjae] ➡ [du-beon-jjae]
two　　　ordinal　　　second time

셋　　　　번째　　　　세번째
[set] + [beon-jjae] ➡ [se-beon-jjae]
three　　　ordinal　　　third time

'처음 [cheo-eum]' is a shortened form of
'첫번째 [cheot-beon-jjae].'

(3) OPPOSITES

Here are some of the affixes with opposite meanings.

좌 [jwa] : left ↔ 우 [u] : right

좌		측		좌측
[jwa]	+	[cheug]	➡	[jwa-cheug]
left		side		left side

좌		회전		좌회전
[jwa]	+	[hwe-jeon]	➡	[jwa-hwe-jeon]
left		turn		left turn

우		회전		우회전
[u]	+	[hwe-jeon]	➡	[u-hwe-jeon]
right		turn		right turn

장 [jang] : long ↔ 단 [dan] : short

장 [jang] long + 점 [jeom] point ➡ 장점 [jang-jjeom]PR1,3 advantage

장 [jang] long + 거리 [geo-ri] distance ➡ 장거리 [jang-geo-ri] long distance

단 [dan] short + 점 [jeom] point ➡ 단점 [dan-jjeom]PR1,3 disadvantage

단 [dan] short + 축 [chug] reduce ➡ 단축 [dan-chug] shorten

고 [go] : high ↔ 저 [jeo] : low

고		품질		고품질
[go]	+	[pum-jil]	➡	[go-pum-jil]
high		quality		high quality

고		소득		고소득
[go]	+	[so-deug]	➡	[go-so-deug]
high		income		high income

저		층		저층
[jeo]	+	[cheung]	➡	[jeo-cheung]
low		floor		low-rise

저		렴		저렴
[jeo]	+	[ryeom]	➡	[jeo-ryeom]
low		frugal		low price

신 [shin] : new ↔ 구 [gu] : old

신 [shin] new + 세대 [se-dae] generation ➡ 신세대 [shin-se-dae] new generation

신 [shin] new + 기 [gi] strange ➡ 신기(하다) [shin-gi-ha-da] amazing

구 [gu] old + 식 [shig] style ➡ 구식 [gu-shig] old style

구 [gu] old + 닥다리 [dag-da-ri] ➡ 구닥다리 [gu-dag-da-ri] outdated

대 [dae] : big ↔ 소 [so] : small

대		박		대박
[dae]	+	[bag]	➡	[dae-bag]
big		ship		jackpot

대		표		대표
[dae]	+	[pyo]	➡	[dae-pyo]
big		represent		representative

소		심		소심
[so]	+	[shim]	➡	[so-shim]
small		heart, mind		timid

소		녀		소녀
[so]	+	[nyeo]	➡	[so-nyeo]
small		female		girl

강 [gang] : strong ⬌ 약 [yag] : weak

강 [gang] strong + 요 [yo] demand ➡ 강요 [gang-yo] pressure

강 [gang] strong + 도 [do] theft, degree ➡ 강도 [gang-do] robber, strength

약 [yag] weak + 점 [jeom] point ➡ 약점 [yag-jeom] weakness

약 [yag] weak + 소 [so] small ➡ 약소 [yag-so] weak and small

남 [nam] : male ⬌ 여(녀) [yeo] : female

남   동생   남동생

[nam] + [dong-saeng] ➡ [nam-dong-saeng]

male   younger sibling   younger brother

남   녀   남녀

[nam] + [nyeo] ➡ [nam-nyeo]

male   female   men and women

여   신   여신

[yeo] + [shin] ➡ [yeo-shin]

female   god   goddess

여   대   여대

[yeo] + [dae] ➡ [yeo-dae]

female   university   women's university

온 [on] : warm ↔ 냉 [naeng] : cold

온 [on] + 기 [gi] ➡ 온기 [on-gi]
warm   atmosphere   warm atmosphere

온 [on] + 도 [do] ➡ 온도 [on-do]
warm   degree   temperature

냉 [naeng] + 수 [su] ➡ 냉수 [naeng-su]
cold   water   cold water

냉 [naeng] + 면 [myeon] ➡ 냉면 [naeng-myeon]
cold   noodle   cold noodle

OPPOSITES

(N) advantage 장점 [jang-jjeom]^{PR1.3}

(N) cold water 냉수 [naeng-su]

(N) disadvantage 단점 [dan-jjeom]^{PR1.3}

(N) high income 고소득 [go-so-deug]

(N) high quality 고품질 [go-pum-jil]

(N) high-rise 고층 [go-cheung]

(N) jackpot 대박 [dae-bag]

(N) left turn 좌회전 [jwa-hwe-jeon]

(N) long distance 장거리 [jang-geo-ri]

(N) low income 저소득 [jeo-so-deug]

(N) low quality 저품질 [jeo-pum-jil]

(N) low-rise 저층 [jeo-cheung]

(N)
new generation   신세대   [shin-se-dae]

(N)
old style   구식   [gu-shig]

(N)
pressure   강요   [gang-yo]

(N)
representative   대표   [dae-pyo]

(N)
right turn   우회전   [u-hwe-jeon]

(N)
robber, strength   강도   [gang-do]

(N)
short distance   단거리   [dan-geo-ri]

(N)
temperature   온도   [on-do]

(N)
timid   소심   [so-shim]

(N)
weakness   약점   [yag-jjeom]PR1.3

(N)
younger brother   남동생   [nam-dong-saeng]

(N)
younger sister   여동생   [yeo-dong-saeng]

EXERCISE

작가	**1**	**a**	journalist
우회전	**2**	**b**	writer
신세대	**3**	**c**	right turn
기자	**4**	**d**	advantage
남동생	**5**	**e**	singer
장점	**6**	**f**	new generation
울보	**7**	**g**	lumberjack
가수	**8**	**h**	crybaby
냉수	**9**	**i**	younger brother
나무꾼	**10**	**j**	cold water

1-b, 2-c, 3-f, 4-a, 5-i, 6-d, 7-h, 8-e, 9-j, 10-g

잠꾸러기 is _____ in English.

욕심쟁이 is _____ in English.

변호사 is _____ in English.

One thing is _____ in Korean.

Second time is _____ in Korean.

Weakness is _____ in Korean.

sleepyhead, grabber, lawyer, 한개, 두번째, 약점

Adrian Perrig

Adrian Perrig is a professor at Swiss Federal Institute of Technology in Zürich (ETH). He earned his Ph.D. degree in Computer Science from Carnegie Mellon University, and spent three years during his Ph.D. degree at the University of California at Berkeley. He received his B.Sc. degree from the Swiss Federal Institute of Technology in Lausanne (EPFL). He is a recipient of the NSF CAREER award in 2004, the Sloan research fellowship in 2006, the Benjamin Richard Teare teaching award in 2011, and the ACM SIGSAC Outstanding Innovation Award in 2013.

Growing up in a small mountain village in Switzerland, Adrian was raised bi-lingual: his mother Heidi raised him in the Bernese Swiss German, and his father spoke the Wallis Swiss German (the dialects are quite distinct, preventing people without experience of the other to effectively communicate). In his childhood, Adrian learned High German, French, and English in primary and secondary school, and later also learned Spanish in college.

Always fascinated by Asian cultures, Adrian initially learned some Mandarin Chinese, but gave it up for the same reason King Sejong invented Hangul: studying Chinese script is a major obstacle! Greatly enjoying his visits to Korea (thanks to his intrepid and witty friend Heejo) and for communicating with his Korean friends, Adrian decided to learn Korean and was ever since hooked to master it.

Miyoung Jung

Miyoung Jung has studied language education, French language and literature, and Chinese language and literature at SungKyunKwan University in Seoul where she also earned her education certificate. While she was teaching at a language school for two years she won an award for the best teacher. She then completed a master degree in International Economics at Yonsei University and University of Zurich.

Thanks to her passion for languages, in addition

to her native Korean she can speak English, French, Chinese, and German. She has always been enjoying learning new languages and cultures. During her volunteering work to teach Korean to foreigners living in Korea she realized how difficult learning Korean is for Westerners and recognized their stumbling blocks. Her insights and experience with teaching languages provided many invaluable contributions for this book.

Heejo Lee

Heejo Lee is a professor at Korea University, Seoul, Korea. He received his BS, MS, Ph.D. degree from POSTECH, Pohang, Korea, and worked as a postdoc at CERIAS, Purdue University from 2000 to 2001. Before joining Korea University, he was at AhnLab, Inc. as a CTO from 2001 to 2003. When Adrian visited Korea at 2009, they found more intuitive ways of learning Korean than most other textbooks explain.

This Korean book project was further developed

while Heejo was a visiting professor at CyLab/CMU, 2010. Meanwhile, he served as an advisor for cyber security in the Philippines (2006), Uzbekistan (2007), Vietnam (2009), Myanmar (2011), Costa Rica (2013) and Cambodia (2015). The cultural experience gained in Asian and American countries gave him a chance to understand the differences between languages and to realize the need of a more intuitive textbook for foreigners to learn Korean, written from the perspective of a non-native Korean speaker.

He grew up near a peach orchard in a countryside village. His parents always supported him and provided a wonderful environment to grow up. As the peach orchard has always been his home of good memories, he decided to dedicate this book toward his parents and the peach orchard.

Yeon Yim

Yeon Yim is a concept designer / motion graphic artist. During and after earning her BFA in Visual Information from Ewha Woman's University and MFA in Film and Digital Media from Hongik University, she participated in several TV shows, commercials, games, theme parks and online services with Gamehi, Nintendo, NC Soft, MBC and MGM by making concept arts and storyboards. She was a winner of Google Korea's Best Blogger Award 2009 in Culture & Art part.

Born in Seoul, she rarely talked during her childhood so that some people thought she may be mute. Her parents, Clara and Chang, wanted to help Yeon open herself up to the world rather than just living with books and films. Thus, they traveled to different places with Yeon during her childhood. When she was a teenager, she started challenging herself with tasks such as talking to strangers, singing songs in public, or walking into a random place to introduce herself—indeed she got her first job by doing so.

With a deep interest in language learning with the power to make someone brave and overcome shyness, she gladly decided to join Adrian's Korean book project when offered by Heejo. She now wants to help others learn her native language with a smile!

Adrian Perrig

2013- 현재 스위스연방취리히공과대학(ETH) 컴퓨터학과 교수, 미래인터넷 SCION 연구
2013 ACM SIGSAC 최고 이노베이션 수상
2011 Benjamin Richard Teare 티칭 어워드 수상
2002-2012 미국 카네기멜론대학 컴퓨터공학과 교수, CyLab 연구소장
2006 Sloan 리서치 펠로우십
2004 NSF CAREER 수상
2004, 2005 IBM 펠로우십
1997-2002 카네기멜론대학 박사
1992-1997 스위스연방로잔공과대학(EPFL) 컴퓨터공학 학사/석사

정미영

2012-2014 연세대학교 국제경제학 석사
2013 취리히 대학교 경제학부 수학
2010-2011 한국어 교육 봉사활동
2010-2012 (주)청담 어학원 강사
2007-2009 IT 업계 근무
2006년 호주 현지회사 인턴
2005년 성균관대학교 프랑스어문학과/중어중문학과 교육학 학사
2015-2016 KOTRA 취리히 무역관 근무

임정연

2008-현재 프리랜스 일러스트레이터, 모션그래픽 아티스트
2011 한국콘텐츠진흥원(KOCCA) '자랑스러운 대한민국' UCC 공모전 입상
2009 Google Korea 선정 문화/예술 분야 베스트블로거
2008 MGM Studio City Korea 기획 U-IT 테마파크 컨셉아티스트
2007 MBC 태왕사신기 VFX팀 컨셉아티스트
2007 NC Soft 'Lineage2 - Kamael' 스토리보드 아티스트
2006 Gamehi 'Sudden Attack - The Last Bullet' 스토리보드 아티스트
2010-2012 홍익대학교 영상디자인과 석사
2003-2007 이화여자대학교 시각디자인과 학사

이희조

2004-현재 고려대학교 정보대학 컴퓨터학과 교수
2015-현재 IoT 소프트웨어보안 국제공동연구센터 센터장
2010-2011 미국 Carnegie Mellon University CyLab 방문교수
2001-2003 안랩 최고기술책임자 (CTO)
2000-2001 미국 Purdue University CERIAS 박사후연구원
1989-2000 POSTECH 컴퓨터공학과 학사/석사/박사
2006-현재 국가 Cyber Security 정책 자문위원
(필리핀,우즈베키스탄,베트남,미얀마,코스타리카,캄보디아)

LEARNING KOREAN
WITH A SMILE(VOCABULARY)

Date of Publication : 10 / JUL / 2016

Authors : Adrian Perrig, Miyoung Jung, Yeon Yim, Heejo Lee

Publisher : Lee Byung Dug

Publish : COOBUG Publishing Co.

Registration Date : 20 / Nov. / 2011

Registration Number : No. 8-349

Address : #913, ILSANVISTA, 49, Gangsun-ro, Ilsanseo-gu
Goyang-si, Gyeonggi-do, KOREA

Tel : 031)908-9152

Fax : 031)908-9153

isbn 978-89-90636-80-5(03710)